Jest Another GOOD CLEAN JOKE BOOK

Bob Phillips

D0324624

HARVEST HOUSE PUBLISHERS
Eugene, Oregon 97402

JEST ANOTHER GOOD CLEAN JOKE BOOK

ISBN 1-56507-450-5

Printed in the United States of America.

98   99   00   01   /   LP   /   10   9   8   7   6   5   4

Dedicated to
John Drake & John Yakligian
who love to laugh
and have a great sense of humor.

ABALONE

Abalone is an expression of disbelief.

ABASHED

A blowhard Air Force major was promoted to colonel and received a brand new office. His first morning behind the desk, an airman knocked on the door and asked to speak to him. The colonel, feeling the urge to impress the young airman, picked up his phone and said:

"Yes, General, thank you. Yes, I will pass that along to the president this afternoon. Yes, good-bye, sir."

Then, turning to the airman he barked, "And what do you want?"

"Nothing important, sir," said the airman. "I just came to install your telephone."

ACUPUNCTURIST

Did you hear about the patient who called his acupuncturist and said, "I have a terrible pain in my side"?

The acupuncturist replied, "Take two thumbtacks and call me in the morning."

ADMIRATION

Our polite recognition of another man's resemblance to ourselves.

ADVANTAGE

Andy: My girlfriend takes advantage of me.

Joe: What do you mean?

Andy: I invited her out to dinner and she asked me if she could bring a date.

AGE

After a serious operation a lady was still in a coma. Her worried husband stood at the foot of her bed. "Well," said the nurse reassuringly, "at least age is on her side."

"She's not so young," said the husband. "She's 45."

At this point the patient moved slightly and quietly but firmly murmured, "44."

• • •

First lady: How old are you?
Second lady: I never tell anyone my age. It keeps changing every minute.

AGING

You can tell you are getting older when your kids study in history what you used to study as current events.

AIRLINES

Did you hear that some airlines are now putting mistletoe at the baggage counter? That way you can kiss your luggage good-bye.

AIRPORT

Have you ever wondered how they can find one tiny fruit fly at the airport, but they can't find your luggage?

ALIMONY

Alimony is bounty from the mutiny.

• • •

Alimony is taxation without representation.

AMEN

The sermon went on and on and on in the heat of the church. At last the minister paused and asked, "What more, my friends, can I say?"

In the back of the church a voice offered earnestly, "Amen!"

ANCHOR

A young naval student was being put through the paces by an old sea captain. "What would you do if a sudden storm sprang up on the starboard?"

"Throw out an anchor, sir."

"What would you do if another storm sprang up aft?"

"Throw out another anchor, sir."

"And if another terrific storm sprang up forward, what would you do?"

"Throw out another anchor."

"Hold on," said the captain. "Where are you getting all those anchors from?"

"From the same place you're getting your storms, sir."

ANTIQUE

Customer: What! Seven hundred dollars for that antique! Last week you only wanted four hundred and fifty dollars.

Dealer: Well, you know how the cost of labor and materials keeps going up.

ANYTHING WRONG?

At a commuter train station a policeman noticed a woman driver bowed over the steering wheel of her car in evident discomfort.

"Is there anything wrong?" said the policeman.

Half crying and half laughing, the woman responded, "For ten years I have driven my husband to the station to catch his train. This morning I forgot him!"

APOLOGY

An apology is politeness too late.

ARCHIVES

Archives is where Noah kept his bees.

ARGUING

Be sure when arguing with a stupid person that he isn't doing the same.

ARMY

Officer: Are you happy now that you're in the Army?

Soldier: Yes, sir.

Officer: What were you before you got into the Army?

Soldier: Much happier.

• • •

First soldier: What did you do in the Army?

Second soldier: I was an eye doctor. My job was to cut the eyes out of potatoes.

ART

"It's no use. Art doesn't listen to me," said a little boy who was praying for a new bike.

"Art who?" asked the boy's mother.

"Art in heaven," came the reply.

ARTIST

An artist decided to buy a new easel. He wasn't too sure what type to get. At the art shop they offered him two—a big one and a small one. He pondered for a while and finally decided on the lesser of two easels.

ARTISTIC TEMPERAMENT

A disease that afflicts amateurs.

ATMOSPHERE

Did you hear about the new restaurant they opened on the moon? It has great food but no atmosphere.

AUSTRALIA

Q: What was the largest island before Australia was discovered?
A: Australia.

AVERAGE

Wife: Scientists claim that the average person speaks about 10,000 words per day.

Husband: Yes, dear, but remember— you are far above average.

BABIES

Q: Why do we dress little girl babies in pink, and boy babies in blue?
A: Because they can't dress themselves.

• • •

A baby is an alimentary canal with a loud voice at one end and no responsibility at the other.

BABY-SITTER

When the father called home, the six-year-old son answered and said, "Don't talk too loud, Dad, the baby-sitter is asleep."

BACH

Did you hear about the dog who played Bach? He was about to be auditioned by a TV producer. The dog's agent warned the producer that this was a very sensitive dog. "You had better listen to him play, because, if you don't, he loses his temper and leaps at you."

The dog started to play. He was awful. The TV producer patiently waited out the performance. When it was over, he declared angrily, "I should have let him attack. I'm sure his Bach is worse than his bite."

BACHELOR

A bachelor is one who never Mrs. a girl.

BAD DRIVER

A bad driver is the guy you run into.

BAGDAD

Bagdad . . . that's what mother did when she met father.

BALANCE THE BOOKS

Bank president: Where's the cashier?
Manager: Gone to the races.
Bank president: Gone to the races during business hours?
Manager: Yes, sir, it's his last chance of making the books balance.

BANK

George: What's the name of your bank?
Wilbur: "Piggy."

• • •

All banks are the same. They have one window at which ten people are standing. Then they have four windows called "Next Window."

BANK ROBBER

Did you hear about the bank robber that shoved a note under the cage gate to the teller? It said, "Put the money in the bag, and don't try anything funny."

The teller wrote out a note and handed it back to the thief. "Straighten your tie. They're taking your picture."

Baptist

Q: When you have 50 people, all of different opinions, what do you have?

A: A Baptist church.

Barber

The customer settled himself and let the barber put the towel around him. Then he told the barber, "Before we start, I know the weather's awful. I don't care who wins the next big fight, and I don't bet on the horse races. I know I'm getting thin on top, but I don't mind. Now get on with it!"

"Well, sir, if you don't mind," said the barber, "I'll be able to concentrate better if you don't talk so much!"

• • •

Did you hear about the man who walked into a barbershop and said,

"Give me a shave—I don't have time to listen to a haircut"?

BARKING DOG

Bob: Don't be afraid of my dog. You know the old proverb, "A barking dog never bites."

Rich: Yes, I know the proverb, and you know the proverb, but does your dog know the proverb?

BATHROOM SCALE

Did you hear about the new bathroom scale they invented? It takes off weight for good intentions.

BEHAVIOR

Father: Do you think it will improve Junior's behavior if we buy him a bicycle?

Mother: No, but it'll spread his behavior over a wider area.

BELCH

Stranger: Sir, how dare you belch before my wife!

Man: Sorry, old pal. I didn't know it was her turn!

BESTSELLER

If you think no evil, see no evil, and hear no evil, the chances are that you'll never write a bestselling novel.

BIG JOHN

A very small, sickly-looking man was hired as a bartender. The saloon owner gave him a word of warning: "Drop everything and run for your life if ever you hear that Big John is on his way to town."

The man worked several months without any problems. Then one day a cowhand rushed in shouting, "Big John is a'comin'," and knocked the small bartender on the floor in his hurry to get out.

Before the bartender had a chance to recover, a giant of a man with a black bushy beard rode into the saloon, through the swinging doors, on the back of a buffalo, and using a rattlesnake for a whip. The man tore the doors off their hinges, knocked over tables, and flung the snake into the corner. He then took

his massive fist and split the bar in half
as he demanded a drink.

The bartender nervously pushed a
bottle at the man. He bit off the top of
the bottle with his teeth and downed the
contents in one gulp, and turned to
leave. Seeing that the man wasn't hurting
anyone, the bartender asked him if he
would like another drink.

"I ain't got no time," the man roared.
"Big John is a'comin' to town."

BIG MONEY

Boy: My uncle is in Leavenworth be-
cause he made big money.
Girl: How much?
Boy: About a third of an inch too big.

BIRD OF PARADISE

A Californian was visiting his Texan
cousin. While walking with the cousin
through a barren section of land, he saw
a funny looking bird flop across the road
in front of them. "What is it?" the
Californian asked.

"It's a bird of paradise," replied his
Texan cousin.

The Californian replied, "Long way
from home, isn't he?"

BLIND

Man: That horse you sold me is almost blind.

Farmer: Well, I told you he was a fine horse but that he didn't look good.

• • •

Lady: My poor fellow, here is a quarter for you. It must be dreadful to be lame, but just think how much worse it would be if you were blind.

Beggar: Yer right, lady. When I was blind, I was always getting counterfeit money.

BLOOMING IDIOTS

Q: What sort of offspring does a stupid florist have?

A: Blooming idiots.

BLOWHARD

Seated next to a blowhard at a U.N. dinner was an Oriental fellow dressed in the robes of one of the Far Eastern countries. The blowhard, attempting to make conversation, leaned over and said: "You like soupee?"

The Oriental fellow nodded his head.

"You like steakee?"

The Oriental nodded again.

As it turned out, the guest speaker at the dinner was our Oriental friend who got up and delivered a beautiful 50-minute address on the U.N. definition of encouragement to self-reliance by under-developed countries of the world. The speech was in flawless Oxford English.

He returned to his place at the head of the table, sat down, turned to his dinner partner, and said: "You like speechee?"

BOOK REPORT

Did you hear about the student who was reprimanded for not having written a book report on a Dickens novel? The student said, "I couldn't help it. We couldn't get the video."

BOOMERANG

Mike: How do you get rid of a boomerang?

Ike: Throw it down a one-way street.

BORE

A tired guest at a formal function spoke to the man next to him: "Gee, this thing is a bore; I'm going to beat it!"

"I would, too," said the man, "but I've got to stay. I'm the host!"

• • •

When there's nothing left to say, a bore is still saying it.

• • •

He has the gift of gab, but he doesn't know how to wrap it up.

• • •

A bore is a person who insists on talking about himself when you want to talk about yourself.

BORING

Did you hear about the man who was speaking and someone in the audience went to sleep during his boring talk? He got so mad that he took the gavel and hit the sleeping man on the head. The sleeper woke up, took a long look at the speaker, and said, "Hit me again. I can still hear you."

BOSS

The one who is early when you are late and late when you are early.

BOWLER

Fred: I've always wanted to be a bowler in the worst way.

Red: Well, you made it.

BRAT

A child who acts like your own but belongs to someone else.

BREATH

Boy: Oh, I can't catch my breath.

Girl: With your breath you should be thankful!

BRIGHT IDEA

An old Chinaman was eating too much rice, especially since he was too frail to work. Because the man had become a burden, the father of the home—the Chinaman's son, determined to get rid of him. He put him in a wheelbarrow, then started up the mountain. The little eight-year-old grandson went along. He was full of questions. His father explained that the grandfather was old and useless, and the only thing they could do was to take him up the mountain and leave him to die. Then the grandson had a bright idea.

"I'm glad you brought me along, Father, because when you're old, I'll know where to take you."

BUBBLE GUM

Q: What do they call a train that carries bubble gum?

A: A chew-chew train.

BUCKET SEATS

The biggest trouble with the bucket seats on the new cars is that not everybody has the same size bucket.

BUFFALO

A big executive boarded a New York–Chicago train. He explained to the porter: "I'm a heavy sleeper, and I want you to be sure and wake me at 3:00 A.M. to get off in Buffalo. Regardless of what I say, get me up, for I have some important business there."

The next morning he awakened in Chicago. He found the porter and really poured it on with abusive language.

After he left, someone said, "How could you stand there and take that kind of talk from that man?"

The porter said: "That ain't nothing. You should have heard what the man said that I put off in Buffalo."

BUSINESS

Did you hear that business was so bad that the Bankruptcy Court just opened a drive-in window?

• • •

I heard that business was so bad that the lobbyists in Washington are using food stamps to bribe congressmen.

CALF

Neighbor: How is your son doing in college?

Father: Well, I felt like Aaron did in the wilderness. "Behold I poured in the gold, and there came out this calf."

CANCER

Cancer is the cure for smoking.

CANDLES

Q: If you had a box of candles and no matches, how would you light them?

A: Why, simply take one candle out of the box—and the box will be a candle lighter.

CAPITAL PUNISHMENT

Q: What is another name for income tax?

A: Capital punishment.

• • •

Did you hear about the woman who was being questioned about jury duty? She said, "I don't believe in capital punishment."

The judge replied, "This is a case about a woman whose husband took some money she was saving for a new dress and lost it betting on the horses."

The woman paused for a moment and then said, "Maybe I can change my mind about capital punishment."

CAR

The loudest noise in the world is the first rattle in your new car.

• • •

Car prices are getting so high that one dealer put a recovery room next to his showroom.

• • •

So far I've paid off three cars ... my doctor's, my dentist's, and my shrink's.

CAR SICKNESS

The feeling you get every month when the payment is due.

CARBURETOR

A man's car stalled on a country road. When he got out to fix it, a cow came along and stopped beside him. "Your trouble is probably in the carburetor," said the cow.

Startled, the man jumped back and ran down the road until he met a farmer. He told the farmer his story.

"Was it a large red cow with a brown spot over the right eye?" asked the farmer.

"Yes, yes," the man replied.

"Oh! I wouldn't listen to Bessie," said the farmer. "She doesn't know anything about cars."

CARDS

A man walked by a table in a hotel and noticed three men and a dog playing cards. The dog was playing with extraordinary performance.

"This is a very smart dog," the man commented.

"Not so smart," said one of the players. "Every time he gets a good hand he wags his tail."

CAREER

Father pacing the floor with a wailing baby in his arms as his wife lies snug in bed: "Nobody ever asks me how I manage to combine marriage and a career."

CARP

Did you hear about the fellow who went carp fishing? As he was about to throw his first cast, his wallet fell out of his pocket into the lake. A carp grabbed the wallet and started to swim away with it.

Suddenly, another carp ate the carp that had eaten the wallet.

Then, yet another, even larger carp came along and swallowed the carp that ate the carp that devoured the wallet.

And that's how carp-to-carp walleting began.

CASH

The other day I wanted to pay somebody cash, and he demanded to see my driver's license.

CAVITY

A cavity is an empty space waiting to be filled with dentist bills.

CEMENT

"You heard my speech, Professor. Do you think it would improve my delivery if I followed the example of Demosthenes and practiced my diction and elocution with pebbles and marbles in my mouth?"

"I would recommend quick-dry cement."

CHAOS

Surgeon: I think the medical profession is the first profession mentioned in the Bible. God made Eve by carving a rib out of Adam.

Engineer: No, engineering was first. Just think of the engineering job it was to create things out of chaos.

Politician: That's nothing! Who do you think created the chaos?

CHEAPSKATE

A very tight man was looking for a gift for a friend. Everything was too expensive except for a glass vase that had been broken, which he could purchase for almost nothing. He asked the store to send it, hoping his friend would think it had been broken in transit.

In due time he received an acknowledgment: "Thanks for the vase," it read. "It was so thoughtful of you to wrap each piece separately."

CHICKEN

Did you hear about the count that stole the king's crown? They tried and tried to make him confess, but he would not. Finally, they said, "We will chop off your head if you don't tell us."

He would not tell them, so they took him to the chopping block. They told him that he would have one more chance, but he did not take it.

As the head chopper started down with the ax, the count said, "All right, I'll tell you." But it was too late . . . his head went rolling to the ground.

Moral: Don't hatchet your counts before they chicken.

CHILDISH GAMES

Childish games are those at which your wife beats you.

CHIMNEY SWEEP

A chimney sweep is a person who does things to soot himself.

CHRONIC FATIGUE

Did you hear that they recently scheduled a seminar on Chronic Fatigue Syndrome. It was a failure. Everybody was too tired to go.

CIGAR

The man bought a cigar in a department store and lit it while still in the store. A clerk told him to put it out because smoking wasn't allowed in the store.

"What do you mean?" he said. "You sell cigars but don't allow smoking?"

"We also sell bath towels," said the girl sweetly.

CIGARETTE

There is a new brand of cigarettes with earplugs in every pack. It's for people who don't want to hear why they should quit smoking.

CLERGYMAN

A clergyman had been invited to attend a party of the Sunday school nursery department. He decided to surprise them. So, getting on his hands and knees, flapping his coattails over his head like wings, he hopped in on all fours, cackling like a bird. Imagine his surprise when he learned that due to a switch in locations, he had intruded on the ladies' missionary meeting!

CLEVER

Did you hear about the inventor who designed a knife that would slice two loaves of bread at the same time? He sold it to a large bakery.

He then developed a knife that could slice three loaves of bread at the same time. He sold that idea too!

Finally, the ultimate. He made a huge knife that could cut four loaves of bread at the same time! And so was born the world's first four-loaf cleaver.

• • •

Three fellows went to church, and when it came time to pass the plate, the three discovered that they had no money. Not wanting to be embarrassed, one fainted and the other two carried him out.

COBWEB

"I heard about an artist who painted a cobweb on the ceiling so realistically that the maid spent hours trying to get it down."

"Sorry, I don't believe it."

"Why not? Artists have been known to do such things."

"Yes, but maids haven't."

COINCIDENCE

First liberal: What does coincidence mean?

Second liberal: Funny, I was going to ask you the same thing!

COLD CUTS

Willard: What's good for cold cuts?
Wallace: Frozen Band-Aids.

COLLECTION

A church function in which many take but a passing interest.

COLLECTOR

Q: What do they call a collector of old magazines?
A: A doctor.

COLLEGE-BRED

College bred is a four-year loaf requiring a fearful amount of dough and is seldom self-raising.

COMPLAINING

Our forefathers did without sugar until the thirteenth century, without coal fires until the fourteenth, without buttered bread until the sixteenth, without tea or soap until the seventeenth, without gas, matches, or electricity until the nineteenth, without cars, or canned or frozen foods until the twentieth. Now, what was it you were complaining about?

• • •

One department store just put in a push-button answering gimmick. If you want to get the mail-order shopping service, you just push #1. If you want to know the price of an object, push #2. If you want to register a complaint, you just press 6666099488477363635255218181818.

CONCEITED

I know a man who is really conceited. He joined the navy so the world could see him.

• • •

I know a man who is very conceited. When he turns away from his mirror, he thinks he's cheating!

CONCLUSION

Our speaker for the evening needs no introduction. What he needs is a conclusion.

CONFIDENCE

A burglar, needing money to pay his income taxes, decided to burgle the safe in a store. On the safe door he was very pleased to find a note reading, "Please don't use dynamite. The safe is not locked. Just turn the knob." He did so.

Instantly a heavy sandbag fell on him, the entire premises were floodlighted, and alarms started clanging. As the police carried him out on a stretcher, he was heard moaning, "My confidence in human nature has been rudely shaken."

CONGRESS

I don't know where we're going to put all the crooks today. The prisons and Congress are full.

• • •

Congress loves to adjourn and go home. I can't understand it. If I were my congressman, I'd be afraid to go home.

• • •

On many issues, Congress is of one mind . . . five hundred congressmen and one mind.

• • •

Some pork-barrel bills are so blatantly stealing that some of the congressmen vote with a stocking on their heads!

• • •

Congressmen have stopped passing the buck. Now, they keep it.

CONSCIENCE

Conscience is that still small voice that tells you the Internal Revenue Service might check your return.

• • •

A conscience is what feels bad while everything else is feeling good.

CONSULTATION

A medical term meaning "share the wealth."

COUNTERFEIT

Counterfit is a seizure you get while paying your bill at the supermarket.

COURAGE

Someday I would like to see a waiter with enough courage to lay the check faceup on the table.

CRAZY

They just redecorated my friend's room. They put new padding on the walls.

• • •

The psychiatrist was matter-of-fact, saying, "After listening to you for so many hours, I must tell you that you are really crazy."

The patient said, "I think I'd like a second opinion."

"All right. You're ugly too!"

• • •

The psychiatrist said sternly to the patient: "If you think you're walking out of here cured after only three sessions, you're crazy."

CREDIT

Even though I owe a fortune, I have a lot to be grateful for. At least I'm not one of my creditors.

• • •

Credit lets you start at the bottom and then dig yourself into a hole.

CREDITORS

Running into debt isn't so bad. It's running into creditors that hurts.

CRIME

My old neighborhood was so bad that when you made a reservation at a restaurant, you requested the "no shooting" section.

• • •

They say that an Indy 500 pit crew can get the tires off a car in 40 seconds.

If they think that's fast, they've never been in Los Angeles.

• • •

In my hometown, you don't have to worry about crime in the streets. They make house calls.

• • •

Crime is growing. When you call the local police, there's now a three-week waiting list.

CRIMINAL LAWYER

Old man: And what do you do, sir?
Lawyer: I'm a criminal lawyer.
Old man: Aren't they all!

CRITIC

One theatrical critic said that he saw a play under unfortunate circumstances—the curtain was up.

CROOK

A crook is a business rival who has just left the room.

CRUISE

The food on the cruise was nice, but all day long people kept bringing it up.

CUPID

Someone once said that Cupid is a lifesaver, but that's ridiculous! He pushes you right into the Sea of Matrimony.

• • •

There is evidence that Cupid is a trapper as well as a hunter.

CURIOSITY

A man sitting at the window one evening casually called to his wife, "There goes that woman Ken Roberts is in love with."

His wife in the kitchen dropped the plate she was drying, ran into the living room, knocked over a vase, and looked out the window. "Where, where?" she said.

"Over there," said the husband. "The woman in the blue dress standing on the corner."

"Why, you big idiot," she replied, "that's his wife."

"Yes, of course," answered the husband with a satisfied grin.

DAY OFF

Nobody is sicker than the man who is sick on his day off.

DEACON

A Baptist deacon had advertised a cow for sale.

"How much are you asking for it?" inquired a prospective purchaser.

"A hundred and fifty dollars," said the advertiser.

"And how much milk does she give?"

"Four gallons a day," he replied.

"But how do I know she will actually give that amount?" asked the purchaser.

"Oh, you can trust me," reassured the advertiser. "I'm a Baptist deacon."

"I'll buy it," replied the other. "I'll take the cow home and bring you back the money later. You can trust me. I'm a Presbyterian elder."

When the deacon arrived home he asked his wife, "What is a Presbyterian elder?"

"Oh," she explained, "a Presbyterian elder is about the same as a Baptist deacon."

"Oh, dear," groaned the deacon, "I have just lost my cow!"

DEBTS

Two men were discussing money when one of them said, "I always manage to put some money away. I never pay my old debts."

"What about the new ones?"

"I let them get old."

DECISIONS

A young man came for an interview with a bank president.

"Tell me, sir, how did you become so successful?"

"Two words."

"And what are they, sir?"

"Right decisions."

"How do you make right decisions?"

"One word . . . experience."

"And how do you get experience?"

"Two words."

"And what are they?"

"Wrong decisions!"

DEMOCRATS

Sunday school teacher: Now, who decreed that all the world should be taxed?

Student: The Democrats.

DENTIST

Did you hear about the man who went to a dentist? During the examination, the man said, "My teeth are great. But let me tell you something. I never brush my teeth. I never use a rinse on my teeth. I never use a breath mint. I eat garlic all day long. And I've never had bad breath."

The dentist replied, "You need an operation."

"What kind of operation?"

"On your nose."

DEPRESSION

Four causes of housewife depression: ABC, NBC, CBS, and FOX.

DERMATOLOGIST

A person who makes rash statements.

DETOUR

The roughest distance between two points.

DIAMOND JUBILEE

A diamond jubilee occurs when the last installment is paid on the engagement ring.

DIET

A short period of starvation preceding a gain of five pounds.

• • •

Have you heard about the great new pasta diet? You walk past a bakery, past a candy store, past an ice-cream shop . . .

• • •

Have you heard about the new garlic diet? You eat nothing but garlic. You don't lose weight, but people stand farther away, and you look thinner from a distance.

DIETER'S PSALM

My weight is my shepherd;
I shall not want low-calorie foods.
It maketh me to munch on potato chips
    and bean dip;
It leadeth me into 31 Flavors;
It restoreth my soul food;
It leadeth me in the paths of cream puffs
    in bakeries.
Yea, though I waddle through the valley
    of weight watchers,
I will fear no skimmed milk;
For my appetite is with me;

My Hostess "Twinkies" and "Ding
   Dongs," they comfort me;
They anointeth my body with calories;
My scale tippeth over!
Surely chubbiness and contentment shall
   follow me
All the days of my life.
And I shall dwell in the house of Marie
   Callender Pies . . . forever!

DINNER

I told my wife I wanted to be surprised at dinner. She surprised me all right. She soaked all the labels off the cans!

• • •

Dinner was a little late at my house yesterday. The pizza truck broke down.

DISHES

Wife: Would you help me with the dishes?

Husband: That isn't a man's job.

Wife: The Bible suggests that it is.

Husband: Where does it say that?

Wife: In 2 Kings 21:13 it says, "And I will wipe Jerusalem as a man wipeth a dish, wiping it and turning it upside down."

DIZZY

Love doesn't really make the world go round. It just makes people dizzy.

DOCTOR

A nurse burst into the doctor's office and said, "Doctor, the patient you just gave a clean bill of health dropped dead outside the door. What should I do?"

The doctor replied, "Quick! Turn him the other way so it'll look like he was just coming in."

• • •

Patient: Can I get a second opinion?
Doctor: Sure. Come back tomorrow.

• • •

I have a very neat doctor. He always washes his hands before he touches my wallet.

• • •

I've found a way of getting my doctor to make a house call. I bought a place on a golf course.

• • •

I had a bad accident, but the doctor told me he'd have me walking again in no time. It was true. I had to sell my car to pay his bill.

• • •

A patient walked into a doctor's office and was told he needed an operation. He asked, "What are you operating for?"

The doctor said, "Two thousand dollars."

The patient said, "No, I meant, what's the reason?"

The doctor said, "I told you—two thousand dollars!"

DOLLAR

One reason the dollar won't do as much for anyone as it used to is that no one will do as much for a dollar as they used to.

DOUBLE TAKE

Life's briefest moment is the time between reading the sign on the freeway and realizing you just missed your exit.

DRAFTSMAN

A draftsman is a husband who leaves windows open.

DRUMS

Mother: I don't think the man upstairs likes Mike to play on his drums.

Father: Why do you say that?

Mother: Because this afternoon he gave Mike a knife and asked him if he knew what was inside the drum.

DULL

One girl to another: "There's never a dull moment when you're out with Donny... it lasts the whole evening."

DUTIES

Duties are tasks we look forward to with distaste, perform with reluctance, and brag about ever after.

EFFECTIVE

Boss: I am planning a salary increase for you, young man.

Employee: When does it become effective?

Boss: Just as soon as you do!

EGOTIST

An egotist is someone who is always me-deep in conversation.

ELEPHANTS

A jeweler watched as a huge truck pulled up in front of his store. The back came down and an elephant walked out. It broke one of the windows with its tusk and then, using the trunk like a vacuum cleaner, sucked up all the jewelry. The elephant then got back into the truck and it disappeared out of sight. When the jeweler finally regained his senses he called the police.

The detectives came, and he told them his story.

"Could you describe the elephant?" one of the detectives said.

"An elephant is an elephant. If you've seen one you've seen them all. What do you mean, 'describe him'?" asked the jeweler.

"Well," said the policeman, "there are two kinds of elephants, African and Indian. The Indian elephant has smaller ears and is not as large as the African elephant."

The jeweler said, "I can't help you out. He had a stocking pulled over his head."

EMBARRASS

Two girls boarded a crowded bus and one of them whispered to the other,

"Watch me embarrass a man into giving me his seat."

Pushing her way through the crowd, she turned all her charms upon a gentleman who looked like he might embarrass easily. "My dear Mr. Wilson," she gushed, "fancy meeting you on the bus. Am I glad to see you. Why, you're almost a stranger. My, but I'm tired."

The sedate gentleman looked up at the girl. He had never seen her before, but he rose and said pleasantly, "Sit down, Mary, my girl. It isn't often I see you on washday. No wonder you're tired. Being pregnant isn't easy. By the way, don't deliver the wash until Thursday. My wife is going to the District Attorney's office to see whether she can get your husband out of jail."

EMBARRASSING

Conceited: I can tell just by looking into a girl's eyes exactly how she feels about me.

Girl: Gee, that must be embarrassing for you.

ENEMY

I don't have an enemy in the world. I outlived them all.

ENGAGEMENT

No, he hasn't sprung the question yet, but his voice sure has an engagement ring in it.

ENGAGEMENT RING

Engrid: Well, what happened when you showed the girls in the office your new engagement ring? Did they all admire it?

Eunice: Better than that, four of them recognized it.

EUREKA

A euphemism for "You smell bad."

EXCUSE ME

A man was walking down some stairs when all of a sudden he slipped. In the process a stout lady toppled against him and they ended up on the bottom step with the lady sitting in the man's lap. The man tapped the lady on the shoulder and said, "I'm sorry, lady," he rasped, "but this is as far as I go."

EXECUTIVE

An executive came home and slumped in his favorite chair with a discouraged look. His wife asked what was wrong.

"You know these aptitude tests we're giving at the office? Well, I took one today for fun. It's a good thing I own the company!"

• • •

An executive is a person who can take two hours for lunch without anybody missing him.

EXERCISE

The only exercise some people get is jumping to conclusions, running down their friends, sidestepping responsibility, and pushing their luck.

• • •

They say exercise kills germs. Have you ever wondered how they get them to exercise?

• • •

I always do my exercises regularly in the morning. Immediately after waking I say sternly to myself, "Ready, now. Up. Down. Up. Down!" And after two strenuous minutes I tell myself, "Okay, boy. Now try the other eyelid."

FAINT

A man rose from his seat in a crowded bus so a lady standing nearby could sit down. She was so surprised she fainted.

When she revived and sat down, she said, "Thanks." Then he fainted.

FALSE TEETH

Speaker: This is terrible! I'm the speaker at this banquet, and I forgot my false teeth!

Man: I happen to have an extra pair; try these.

Speaker: Too small!

Man: Well, try this pair.

Speaker: Too big!

Man: I have one pair left.

Speaker: These fit just fine. It sure is lucky to sit next to a dentist!

Man: I'm not a dentist. I'm an undertaker.

FAMOUS LAST WORDS

This is General Custer speaking. Men, don't take prisoners!

FANCY

I shop in a very fancy department store. The salesclerks there ignore you by appointment only.

FARMER

Once upon a time there lived a farmer who owned a big hay field. The farmer's son decided to move to the city and earn his living there. But when he got to the city, the best he could do was get a job as a bootblack at the railroad station. Now the farmer makes hay while the son shines.

FAST

Speeder: But, Judge, I do everything fast.

Judge: Let's see how fast you can do 30 days.

FAST-FOOD

Some fast-food companies are starting to hire older people. Now you can make as much at 80 as you did when you were 14!

FAST LEARNER

A little prospector wearing clean new shoes walked into a saloon. A big Texan said to his friend standing at the bar, "Watch me make this dude dance."

He walked over to the prospector and said, "You're a foreigner, aren't you? From the East?"

"You might say that," the little prospector answered. "I'm from Boston and I'm here prospecting for gold."

"Now tell me something. Can you dance?"

"No, sir. I never did learn to dance."

"Well, I'm going to teach you. You'll be surprised how quickly you can learn."

With that, the Texan took out his gun and started shooting at the prospector's feet. Hopping, skipping, and jumping, the little prospector was shaking like a leaf by the time he made it to the door.

About an hour later the Texan left the saloon. As soon as he stepped outside the door, he heard a click. He looked around and there, four feet from his head, was the biggest shotgun he had ever seen.

The little prospector said, "Mr. Texan, have you ever kissed a mule?"

"No," said the quick-thinking Texan, "but I've always wanted to."

FATHER'S DAY

Father's Day scares me. I'm afraid they'll get me something I can't afford.

FERN

A fern is a plant you're supposed to water once a day. When you don't, it dies. But if you do, it dies anyway, only not so soon.

FILING CABINET

A useful container where things can be lost alphabetically.

FLABBERGASTED

The state you get in when you're over-whelmed by a flabber.

FLATTERER

A slanderer is someone who says things behind your back he wouldn't say to your face.

A flatterer is someone who says things to your face he wouldn't say behind your back.

FLAT TIRE

Man: How far is it to the next filling station?

Farmer: Nigh unto two miles as the crow flies.

Man: Well, how far is it if the crow has to walk and roll a flat tire?

FLOODED

Wife: Honey, I can't get the car started. I think it's flooded.
Husband: Where is it?
Wife: In the swimming pool.
Husband: It's flooded.

FODDER

The man who married Mudder.

FOOTBALL

Neighbor: I understand your son is on the football team. What position does he play?
Father: I think he's one of the drawbacks.

FORGERY

Did you hear about the felon who was charged with forgery? He said, "Judge, I can't even sign my own name."
The judge replied, "You're not charged with signing your own name."

FORTUNE

Did you hear about the two young women who were walking through a meadow when they passed a large bullfrog? Suddenly the frog spoke. "Kiss me, I'm a lawyer."

Without a moment's hesitation, one of the women reached down, picked up the frog, dropped him in her knapsack, and started walking on. The other woman looked at her.

"Aren't you going to kiss him and turn him back?"

"Are you kidding," sneered the first. "Lawyers are a dime a dozen, but a talking frog will make me a fortune!"

• • •

A man was about to take the next plane to Denver when he saw a scale. He put in a quarter and a message came: "You weigh 175 and you're on the way to Denver."

Puzzled, the man put in another quarter, and the same message came out.

Really addled, he went into the men's room, combed his hair in a different way, and changed his sport jacket. He returned and tested the machine with another quarter.

This time the message was: "You still weigh 175, and you just missed your plane to Denver."

FORTUNETELLER

Q: What do you call a midget fortune-teller who escapes from the police?

A: A small medium at large.

FREEDOM

The ability to do what you please without considering anyone except your wife, the police, your boss, your life insurance company, the neighbors, and, the state, federal, and city authorities.

FREEWAY

There is a growing sentiment that the national flower should be a concrete cloverleaf.

GAMBLING

A great way of getting nothing for something.

GANGSTER

Things are getting so bad in my neighborhood that one gangster does all his holdups in daylight. He's afraid to be out on the street at night with all that money.

GARAGE SALE

I was at a garage sale and wanted to buy an item that was marked three dollars. I said, "Fifty cents."

The seller said, "Two-seventy-five."

"Sixty."

"Two-fifty."

"One."

"Two-twenty-five."

"One-twenty-five."

"You know, this is a good game," the seller said. "Let's play a nickel a hundred."

•   •   •

Did you hear about the woman who picked up a piece of junk at a garage-sale table and asked how much it was? The man of the house said, "A penny."

"That's too much."

"Okay, make me an offer."

•   •   •

A garage sale is a technique for distributing all the junk in your garage among all the other garages in the neighborhood.

GERONIMO

Did you hear about the man who jumped from the Empire State Building and lived to tell about it? He told the people on the 93rd floor, those on the 84th floor, everyone on the 62nd floor, and those on . . .

GET-UP-AND-GO

It's nice to see people with plenty of get-up-and-go, especially if some of them are visiting you.

GIRDLE MANUFACTURER

A girdle manufacturer is a fellow who lives off the fat of the land.

GIVING

Did you hear about the town's richest man who met with the minister after the Sunday service? "Why does everyone call me cheap and stingy?" complained the man. "I've told everyone I'm leaving half my money to the church when I die."

The minister nodded. "It reminds me of the story about the pig and the cow. The cow was much loved by the farmer and his neighbors, while the pig was not popular at all. The pig could not understand this and asked the cow about it. 'How come you are so well-liked, cow? People say you're generous and good because you give milk and butter and cream every day. But I give more than that. From me they get bacon and ham; they even pickle my feet. Yet I'm not popular and you are. Why do you think that is?' The cow looked down at the pig and answered, 'Perhaps it's because I give while I'm still alive.' "

GLACIERS

"Dear me," said the old lady on a visit to the mountains, "look at all those big rocks. Where did they all come from?"

"The glaciers brought them down," said the guide.

"But where are the glaciers?"

"The glaciers," said the guide in a weary voice, "have gone back for more rocks."

GOING OUT OF BUSINESS

Going out of business has become so profitable for one merchant that he's opening a chain of going-out-of-business stores.

GOLF

First golfer: Pardon me, but would you mind if I played through?

Second golfer: I guess not, but why?

First golfer: I've just heard that my wife has been taken seriously ill.

• • •

A pastor and one of his parishioners were playing golf at a local country club. It was a very close match. At the last hole, the pastor teed up, addressed the ball, and swung his driver with great force. The ball stubbornly rolled off the tee and settled slowly some 12 feet away instead of sailing down the fairway.

The clergyman frowned, glared after the ball, and bit his lip, but said nothing.

His opponent regarded him for a moment and sighed, "Pastor, that is the most profane silence I have ever heard!"

• • •

Two men were beginning a game of golf. The first man stepped to the tee, and his first drive gave him a hole-in-one. The second man stepped up to the tee and said, "Okay, now I'll take my practice swing, and then we'll start the game."

• • •

Golf is great exercise, especially climbing in and out of the cart.

• • •

Q: What is the biggest handicap in golf?

A: Honesty.

GOOD CATCH

One of the unmarried girls who works in a busy office arrived early the other morning and began passing out cigars and candy, both tied with blue ribbons. When asked what the occasion was, she proudly displayed a diamond solitaire on her third finger, left hand, and announced: "It's a boy... six feet tall and 187 pounds."

GOOD FOR SOCIETY

Judge: What good have you ever done for society?

Robber: Well, I've kept four or five detectives working regularly.

GOSSIP

One gossip was overheard saying to a friend, "You know I only say good things about people. Well, this is good..."

GOTCHA

Gina: I've never seen Gail look so pale.
Gloria: She was probably out in the rain without an umbrella.

• • •

Two married girls were bothering a third girl who was still a spinster. "Now, tell us truthfully," they badgered her, "have you ever really had a chance to marry?"

With a withering glance, she retorted, "Suppose you ask your husbands."

GOVERNMENT

Every time my ship comes in, the government unloads it.

• • •

Did you hear about the young man who applied for a government job? When asked what he could do, he said, "Nothing."

He got the job immediately. They figured they wouldn't have to break him in!

GRANDPARENT

Q: What is the name for an older person who keeps your mother from spanking you?

A: A grandparent.

GRASS HOUSE

Did you hear about the tribe in Africa that stole the king's throne from a rival tribe? They hid the throne in the rafters of their grass hut. The men who stole the throne were having a party in the hut. They were feeling happy about their successful theft when all of a sudden the rafters broke and the throne fell down and killed all of the men.

Moral: Those who live in grass houses shouldn't stow thrones.

GRAVE

Two men took a shortcut through a graveyard and noticed a gravestone that read, "Here lies a liberal and a good man."

"Imagine that!" said the one to the other. "I had no idea you could bury two men in one grave!"

GROUCH

Grant: My wife has been nursing a grouch all week.

Graham: Been laid up, have you?

GROWING OLD

Gomer: Did you notice how pleased Mrs. Grave looked when I told her she didn't look a day older than her daughter?

Gabe: I didn't notice Mrs. Grave . . . I was too busy watching the expression on the daughter's face!

• • •

Husband: Dear, do you remember John Williams? He was the student body president at our high school. I saw him today.

Wife: That was 35 years ago.

Husband: I know. In fact, he has gotten so bald and fat that he didn't even recognize me.

GROWING UP

My son is really growing up. Only last week he was able to go to the psychiatrist all by himself.

GUESTS

The most embarrassing moment in one housewife's life was when she happened to be entertaining very special guests. After looking over all the appointments carefully, she put a note on the guest towels, "If you use these I will murder you." It was meant for her husband. In the excitement she forgot to remove the note. After the guests departed, the towels were discovered still in perfect order, as well as the note itself.

HALF-WIT

A person who spends half his time thinking up wisecracks and definitions.

HAMMER FROM SEARS

A man was sitting in a café when all of a sudden someone came in and beat him up. When he woke up he said to the owner, "Who was that?"

"That was Kung Fu from China," replied the owner.

The next week the man was eating in the same café when a different person entered and beat him up. When he woke up he said to the owner, "Who was that?"

The owner said, "That was Kuang Chow from Taiwan."

Several weeks later Kung Fu and Kuang Chow were eating in the café. The man who had been beaten by both of them entered and paid them back the abuse. He said to the owner, "When they wake, tell them that was 'a hammer from Sears'."

HAPPINESS

Happiness is when you see a double chin on your husband's old girlfriend.

HAPPY

He: Will you marry me?
She: No.
He: And they lived happily ever after!

HARI-KARI

Hari-Kari is what happens when you are transporting a wig from one place to another.

HEALTH

I've got so many aches and pains right now that a new one would have to wait about a week before I could feel it.

HELP YOURSELF

Hank: Say, Mr. Hannah, we helped ourselves to some of your apples.

Mr. Hannah: That's okay. I helped myself to some of the tools in your car while you were in the orchard.

HIGH SOCIETY

The following conversation was overheard at a party attended by high society people:

"My ancestry goes all the way back to Alexander the Great," said one lady. She then turned to a second lady and said, "And how far does your family go back?"

"I don't know," was the reply. "All of our records were lost in the Flood."

HISS

The entire audience was hissing him except one man. He was applauding the hissing.

HOBBIES

My wife has two hobbies—she swims and knits. It makes the wool a little soggy, but it keeps her happy.

HOLD IT

Two sailors were adrift on a raft in the ocean. They had just about given up hope of rescue. One began to pray, "O Lord, I've led a worthless life. I've been unkind to my wife, and I've neglected my children, but if you'll save me, I promise..."

The other shouted, "Hold it. I think I see land."

HOLLYWOOD

In Hollywood a successful marriage is when the couple leaves the church together.

HONEST

Policeman: In the gun battle a bullet struck my head and went into space.
Wife: Well, at least you're honest.

HONESTY

A man returned to his sports car to find a freshly crushed fender and this note affixed to his windshield wiper: "The people who saw me sideswipe your fender are now watching me write this note, and doubtless figure I'm telling you my name and address so you can contact me and send me the bill. Ho! Ho! You should live so long."

HORSE DOCTOR

A horse doctor is any horse that graduated from medical school.

HORSE SENSE

Horse sense is what makes horses never bet on people.

HOURS

Applicant: Before I take this job, tell me, are the hours long?
Employer: No, only 60 minutes each.

HOUSEWARMING

Housewarming is the last call for wedding presents.

HOUSEWIFE

The best way for a housewife to get a few minutes to herself at the end of the day is to start doing the dishes.

HOWLING SUCCESS

A howling success is the baby that always gets picked up.

HUCK & FINN

Finn and Huck were friends. Finn up and died. No one was worried, however. They said, "Huck'll bury Finn."

HUNGRY

"I never eat any food with additives. I don't eat anything with preservatives or anything that's been sprayed or anything that's been fed chemical grain."

"And how do you feel?"

"Hungry."

HUNTER

A duck hunter, proud of his marksmanship, took a friend one morning to witness his skill. After some time, a lone duck flew by.

"Watch this," whispered the hunter, as he took careful aim and fired. The duck flew serenely on.

"My boy," said the hunter, "you are witnessing a great miracle. There flies a dead duck."

●   ●   ●

Two hunters bedded down at their campfire and were about to fall asleep when a giant bear loomed in front of them. One hunter rushed to put on his sneakers. The other said, "What good'll that do? You'll never outrun that bear."

The first one said, "All I have to do is outrun you!"

HUNTING

Two dummies went on a hunting trip. Each bagged a moose. Returning to the plane, they were told by the pilot, "Those moose are too heavy. The plane will crash."

One of the dummies said, "We brought two of them in the plane last year."

The pilot shrugged his shoulders and they took off. In ten minutes, the heavy load caused the plane to go down in the woods. One of the dummies said, "This is really something. This is the same place we crashed last year."

IDEAS

A noted American journalist on a trip to China was asked to speak before a Chinese audience. He accepted the invitation. He was about halfway through his speech when he noticed a Chinese man in a corner writing on a blackboard. He became interested and as he spoke he watched the writer who was writing in Chinese. The writer wrote less and less, however, and finally stopped completely. When he had finished speaking, the journalist asked the chairman what the writer had been doing.

"Why," said the chairman, "he was interpreting your speech for the benefit of the members of the audience who do not understand English."

"But," said the speaker, "for the last 20 minutes he did not put anything down."

"Oh," said the chairman, "he was only writing the ideas on the blackboard."

IDIOT

Ingrid: You're not smart enough to talk to an idiot!

Ian: Okay! I'll send you a letter!

• • •

Q: What do they call a fellow who introduces his best girl to his best friend?

A: An idiot.

IMAGINATION

Employer: Look here! What did you mean by telling me you had five year's experience when you've never even had a job before!

Man: Well, you advertised for a man with imagination!

I'M FINE

I'm fine, I'm fine.
There's nothing whatever the matter
    with me,

I'm just as healthy as I can be.
I have arthritis in both of my knees,
And when I talk, I talk with a wheeze.
My pulse is weak and my blood
    is thin,
But I'm awfully well for the shape
    I'm in.
My teeth eventually will have to
    come out,
And I can't hear a word unless you
    shout.
I'm overweight and I can't get thin,
But I'm awfully well for the shape
    I'm in.
Arch supports I have for my feet,
Or I wouldn't be able to walk down
    the street.
Sleep is denied me every night,
And every morning I'm really a sight.
My memory is bad and my head's
    a-spin,
And I practically live on aspirin.
But I'm awfully well for the shape
    I'm in.
The moral is, as this tale unfolds,
That for you and me who are grow-
    ing old,
It's better to say, "I'm fine," with
    a grin

Than to let people know the shape
we're in!

IMPROVEMENT

Q: Which is the largest room in the
world?
A: The room for improvement.

INSANE

A modern murderer is supposed to be
innocent until proven insane.

INSANE ASYLUM

Q: Why do they put people into the
insane asylum?
A: For no reason at all.

INSANITY

Judge: What possible excuse can you
have for freeing this defendant?
Juror: Insanity.
Judge: All 12 of you?

• • •

Irene: Who is that strange looking
man who keeps staring at me?
Ivan: Oh, that's Mr. Inns, the famous
expert on insanity.

INTERNATIONAL CONSCIENCE

The still small voice that tells a country when another country is stronger.

INTRODUCTION

You have heard it said before that this speaker needs no introduction. Well, I have heard him and he needs all the introduction he can get.

• • •

Introducing a speaker:
"There isn't anything I wouldn't do for Mr. _____, and there isn't anything he wouldn't do for me. That's why we have gone through life not doing anything for each other."

IRS

Did you hear about the man who had untold wealth? That's what the IRS got him for.

• • •

I told my IRS auditor, "You can't get blood out of a turnip."
He answered, "No, but we can send the turnip to jail."

• • •

I went to the IRS last week and really let them have it. Every penny I had.

JEALOUSY

Q: What do they call the friendship that one movie actor has for another?
A: Jealousy.

JOGGING

Since jogging came along, more people are collapsing in perfect health.

JOINT CHECKING ACCOUNT

A device that permits the wife to beat the husband to the draw.

JOKE

Judge: Did you steal this man's television set?
Thief: Oh, I only took it for a joke.
Judge: How far did you carry it?
Thief: From his house to mine . . . about three miles.
Judge: Six months in jail. That was carrying a joke too far.

• • •

A boss called the entire office staff together and told them a new joke.

Everyone but one man laughed uproariously.

"What's the matter?" grumbled the boss. "Don't you have a sense of humor?"

"I don't have to laugh," said the man. "I'm leaving Friday anyhow."

JONESES

Now I know why I could never keep up with the Joneses. They were just indicted for tax evasion.

• • •

I found out why it's so hard to keep up with the Joneses. They're on welfare.

JUDGE

Did you hear about the convicted felon who jumped up in court and said, "How do you like that? Twelve people out of 250 million find me guilty. And you call that justice. As God is my judge," he yelled out, "I'm not guilty."

The judge said, "He's not. I am. Six years!"

JUNK

Junk is the stuff we throw away. Stuff is the junk we save.

• • •

Junk is something you keep ten years and then throw away two weeks before you need it.

JURY DUTY

Just think of it this way... when you're on trial, your fate is being settled by 12 people who weren't smart enough to get out of jury duty.

KAMIKAZE

First pilot: I was a Kamikaze flier during the war. My name was Chow Mein.

Second pilot: How could that be? That was a suicide squad.

First pilot: Oh, they called me Chicken Chow Mein.

KINGDOM

Kingdom is what they call a king who isn't very bright.

KING MIDAS

Q: Who was King Midas?

A: He was the Greek king who fixed chariot mufflers.

KISS

Father: When I was your age, I never kissed a girl. Will you be able to tell your children that?

Son: Not with a straight face.

• • •

Him: If I tried to kiss you, would you call for help?

Her: Do you need help?

• • •

Mother: If a young man asks you for a kiss, refuse it.

Daughter: And if he doesn't ask for it?

• • •

Girl: Did you kiss me when the lights were out?

Boy: No!

Girl: It must have been that fellow over there!

Boy (starting to get up): I'll teach him a thing or two!

Girl: You couldn't teach him a thing!

• • •

Kent: Your little brother just saw me kiss you. What can I give him to keep him from telling?

Katie: He generally gets a dollar.

KISSING

Kissing shortens life—single life.

KITE

I bought my kid a kite and he went crazy. He couldn't find where to put the batteries.

KNOCK, KNOCK

Knock, knock.
Who's there?
Major.
Major who?
Major ask, didn't I?

• • •

Knock, knock.
Who's there?
Hume.
Hume who?
Hume do you expect.

• • •

Knock, knock.
Who's there?
Summertime.
Summertime who?
Summertime I'm going to stop telling knock-knock jokes.

• • •

Knock, knock.
Who's there?
Sherwood.
Sherwood who?
Sherwood like to hear another knock-knock joke.

• • •

Knock, knock.
Who's there?
Stella.
Stella who?
Stella nother crazy knock-knock joke.

• • •

Would you know me if you didn't see me for a day?
Sure!
Knock, knock.
Who's there?
See! You've forgotten me already.

LAPLANDER

Someone who jumps onto other people's laps.

LATE

Jones came into the office an hour late for the third time in one week and found the boss waiting for him. "What's the story this time, Jones?" he asked sarcastically. "Let's hear a good excuse for a change."

Jones sighed, "Everything went wrong this morning, boss. The wife decided to drive me to the station. She got ready in ten minutes, but then the drawbridge got stuck. Rather than let you down, I swam across the river (look, my suit's still damp), ran out to the airport, got a ride on Mr. Thompson's helicopter, landed on top of Radio City Music Hall, and was carried here piggyback by one of the Rockettes."

"You'll have to do better than that, Jones," said the boss, obviously disappointed. "No woman can get ready in ten minutes."

• • •

Every day Mr. Lane's secretary was 20 minutes late. Then one day she slid snugly into place at her desk only five minutes tardy.

"Well," said Mr. Lane, "this is the earliest you've ever been late."

• • •

Q: What is the most effective way to turn people's heads?
A: Go to church late.

LATIN

Q: Name an outstanding feat of the Romans.

A: Speaking Latin.

LAUGH

Man: What would you say if I asked you to be my wife?

Woman: Nothing. I can't talk and laugh at the same time.

LAUGHTER

Q: What remedy is there for someone who splits his side with laughter?

A: Have him run as fast as he can—till he gets a stitch in his side.

LAWYER

I met a lawyer at a party and asked him about a problem I was having, and inquired whether I needed a lawyer. He billed me for a hundred bucks the next day. I asked another lawyer friend if he could do that, and this lawyer billed me for two hundred.

• • •

The fence between heaven and hell fell down. Appearing at the broken section, Saint Peter called to Satan, "Look, since you've got all the engineers on your side, why don't you get some of them to repair this fence?"

Satan said, "Are you kidding? My men are much too busy."

"I'll have to sue you."

"Think so? Where are you going to get a lawyer?" Satan asked.

• • •

A crook just arrived back from a robbery, and a friend asked: "What did you get?"

Crook: It was a lawyer's house.

Friend: Oh, then what did you lose?

• • •

Judge: How is it that you can't get a lawyer to defend you?

Defendant: As soon as they found out I didn't steal the million, they quit!

LENDING

Never lend money. It gives people amnesia.

LIBERAL

Removing a conscience from a liberal is classified as a minor operation.

LIBRARIAN

Q: When a librarian goes fishing, what does she use for bait?
A: Bookworms.

LIFE INSURANCE

The thing that keeps you poor all your life so you can die rich.

• • •

Q: What's the quickest way to collect on your life insurance?
A: Tell a hippo his mother wears combat boots.

LIVING ROOM

Q: What did the man do when he heard he was going to die?
A: He went into the living room.

LOCOMOTIVE

A ridiculous reason for doing something.

LORD'S PRAYER

Children's versions of the Lord's Prayer:

• Our Father, Who are in heaven, hello!
What be Thy name?

- Give us this day our daily breath.

- Our Father, Who are in heaven,
  Hollywood be Thy name.

- Our Father, Who are in heaven, Harold
  be Thy name.

- Give us this day our jelly bread.

- Lead us not into creation.

- Deliver us from weevils.

- Deliver us from eagles.

LOUDER

During a long lecture a speaker suffered many interruptions from a man in the balcony who kept yelling, "Louder! Louder!"

After about the fifth interruption, a gentleman in the first row stood up, looked back, and asked, "What's the matter, my friend, can't you hear?"

"No, I can't," came the answer from the balcony.

"Well, then, be thankful and shut up!"

LOVE

Love is blind, and marriage is an eye-opener.

LUNATICS

Son: How do they catch lunatics, Dad?

Dad: With lipstick, beautiful dresses, and pretty smiles.

MAP

A map is something that will tell you everything except how to fold it up again.

MARBLES

In order to become a good speaker you must go to diction school. They teach you how to speak clearly. To do this they fill your mouth with marbles and you're supposed to talk clearly right through the marbles. Now, every day you lose one marble. When you've lost all your marbles . . .

MARGIE

Guy: Margie, I love you! I love you, Margie!

Gal: In the first place, you don't love me. In the second place, my name isn't Margie.

MARK

I have a friend who made his mark in the world. That's because he can't write.

MARRIAGE

A man is incomplete until he's married... then he's finished.

• • •

Keep your eyes open before marriage . . . half shut afterwards.

• • •

Martha: When are you thinking about getting married?
Mary: Constantly.

• • •

America still has more marriages than divorces, proving that preachers can still out-talk lawyers.

• • •

To err is human; to blame it on your spouse is even more human.

• • •

Marriage is like horseradish . . . men praise it with tears in their eyes.

• • •

Son: Why is a man not allowed to have more than one wife?

Father: Because the law protects those who are incapable of protecting themselves.

• • •

Marriage is like a railroad sign—first you stop, then you look, then you listen.

• • •

Marriage is like a midnight phone call—you get a ring, and then you wake up.

• • •

Mary: See that woman over there? She's been married four times—once to a millionaire, then to an actor, third to a minister, and last to an undertaker.

Mark: I know! One for the money, two for the show, three to get ready, and four to go.

Marry

She: Do you know why I won't marry you?

He: I can't think.
She: You guessed it right away.

• • •

He: What would you say if I asked you to marry me?
She: Nothing. I can't talk and choke at the same time.

MATRIMONY

A minister forgot the name of a couple he was going to marry, so he said from the pulpit, "Will those wishing to be united in holy matrimony please come forward after the service." After the service, 13 old maids came forward.

MEDICARE

A sample of what might happen if we had socialized medicine is currently making the rounds. It goes something like this:

A man, feeling the need of medical care, went to the medical building. Upon entering the front door, he found himself faced with a battery of doors, each marked with the names of ailments such as appendicitis, heart disease, cancer, and so on.

He felt sure his trouble could be diagnosed as appendicitis, so he entered the door so marked. Upon entering, he found himself faced with two more doors, one marked male and the other female. He entered the door marked male and found himself in another corridor where there were two doors, one marked Protestant and the other Catholic.

Since he was a Protestant, he entered the proper door and found himself facing two more doors, marked taxpayer and nontaxpayer. He still owned equity in his home, so he went through the door marked taxpayer, and found himself confronted with two more doors marked single and married.

He had a wife at home, so he entered the proper door and once more there were two more doors, one marked Republican and the other Democrat.

Since he was a Republican he entered the door and fell nine floors to the alley.

MEGAVITAMINS

Now they have megavitamins. Chew one bottle and you get enough strength to open the second bottle.

Melody in F

Feeling footloose and frisky, a feather-
brained fellow
Forced his fond father to fork over the
farthings
And flew far to foreign fields,
And frittered his fortune feasting fabu-
lously with faithless friends.
Fleeced by his fellows in folly, and facing
famine,
He found himself a feed-flinger in a
filthy farmyard.
Fairly famishing, he fain would've filled
his frame
With foraged food from fodder
fragments.
"Phooey, my father's flunkies fare far
finer,"
The frazzled fugitive forlornly fumbled,
frankly facing facts.
Frustrated by failure, and filled with
foreboding,
He fled forthwith to his family.
Falling at his father's feet, he forlornly
fumbled,
"Father, I've flunked,
And fruitlessly forfeited family fellowship
favor."
The farsighted father, forestalling further
flinching,
Frantically flagged the flunkies to

Fetch a fatling from the flock and fix
    a feast.
The fugitive's faultfinding brother
    frowned
On fickle forgiveness of former folderol.
But the faithful father figured,
"Filial fidelity is fine, but the fugitive is
    found!
What forbids fervent festivity?
Let flags be unfurled! Let fanfares flare!"
Father's forgiveness formed the foun-
    dation
For the former fugitive's future fortitude!

MEMORY

Did you know there are three kinds of
memory...good, bad, and convenient.

MERITS

In Colorado a mining claim was pend-
ing before a judge with a reputation for
a free and easy brand of justice. One
morning his Honor remarked: "Gentlemen, this court has in hand a check from
the plaintiff in this case for $10,000 and a
check from the defendant for $15,000.
The court will return $5,000 to the
defendant. Then we will try the case
strictly on its merits."

MIDDLE-AGED

You know you're middle-aged when your idea of unwinding on a Friday night is to go to bed and read.

MIND

Mike: I believe I could write like Shakespeare if I had a mind to try it.

Michele: Yes, nothing is wanting but the mind!

MINISTER

Delivering a speech at a banquet on the night of his arrival in a large city, a visiting minister told several anecdotes he expected to repeat at meetings the next day. Because he wanted to use the jokes again, he requested that the reporters omit them from any accounts they might turn in to their newspapers. A cub reporter, in commenting on the speech, ended his piece with the following: "The minister told a number of stories that cannot be published."

• • •

Mother: Quick, Marty, call the doctor. Matt just swallowed a coin.

Father: I think we ought to send for the minister. He can get money out of anybody.

• • •

Wife: Who was that at the door, dear?

Husband: It was that new minister. He has been by four times this week.

Wife: What is his name?

Husband: I think it's Pester Smith.

• • •

Ministers fall into four categories:

1. Those who do not have any notes and the people have no idea how long he will speak.

2. Those who put on the podium before them each page of the sermon as they read it. These honest ones enable the congregation to keep track of how much more is to come.

3. Those who cheat by putting each sheet of notes under the others in their hand.

4. And, worst of all, those who put down each sheet of notes as they read them and then horrify the congregation by picking up the whole batch and reading off the other side.

MISERABLE

Maggie: You know, girls, a lot of men are going to be miserable when I marry.

Girls: Really? How many men are you going to marry?

MONKEY

Mike: What's the difference between debating with a monkey and debating with a liberal?

Martha: You get more rational arguments from the monkey.

MONOLOGUE

Son: What is a monologue, Dad?

Dad: That's a conversation between a husband and a wife.

Son: But our teacher said that was a dialogue.

Dad: Your teacher isn't married, son.

MOON

Father: Maty, what are you doing out there?

Maty: I'm looking at the moon.

Father: Well, tell the moon to go home. It's halfpast eleven.

Mountain Climbing

Max looked up at the steep icy mountainside. "I can't do it," he said.

His companions begged him to climb the mountain with them. But he refused to move. "I'm against mountain climbing," he said.

Now they call him "Anti-climb-Max."

Mousetrap

Young wife: Don't forget to bring home another mousetrap.

Husband: What's the matter with the one I brought yesterday?

Young wife: It's full!

Movers and Shakers

Did you know that the world's greatest movers and shakers are those people who just moved into the apartment above you?

Movie Theater

In a movie theater you can still find the cops on the screen. But the crooks are behind the refreshment stand.

MUGGERS

The Los Angeles muggers are up-to-date. They've even started taking credit cards.

MUGWUMP

A person who sits on a political fence with his mug on one side and his wump on the other.

MUSIC

Q: Is it possible to stretch music so that it will last a little longer?

A: Yes, if you have a rubber band.

MY WIFE

I can't understand my wife. She spends two hours with a tweezer, plucking out her eyebrows. Then she spends another two hours with an eyebrow pencil filling them in.

● ● ●

First man: Whenever I have a fight with my wife, she becomes historical.

Second man: You mean—hysterical.

First man: No, historical. She keeps bringing up the past.

NAPOLEON

The whole staff at the mental hospital spent months working on Phillips, who believed he was Napoleon. Finally, the head psychiatrist said to Phillips, "You're all better."

Phillips replied, "Can I make a call? I want to tell Josephine the good news."

NARROW ESCAPE

She was going to have an announcement party, but the engagement was broken, so she went ahead and called it a narrow-escape party.

NATURAL

Photographer (to young man): It will make a much better picture if you put your hand on your father's shoulder.

Father: It would be much more natural if he had his hand in my pocket.

NATURE

Son: Why do they refer to nature as a woman, Dad?

Father: Because they can't find out how old it is, son.

NEATNESS

First woman: I think he might carry neatness too far.

Second woman: What makes you say that?

First woman: Who else do you know that irons his shoelaces?

NERVE

Nick: I hear the groom ran away from the altar.

Nathan: Lost his nerve, I suppose?

Nick: No, found it again.

NERVOUS

Nancy: Were you nervous when George proposed?

Nichole: No, dear, that's when I stopped being nervous.

NERVOUS BREAKDOWN

"To tell the truth, Doctor," said a hard-working housewife, "I've always wanted to have a nervous breakdown. But every time I was about to get around to it, it was time to fix somebody a meal."

NEWLYWEDS

Q: What's the most common cause of death for newlyweds?

A: Eating at home.

NICKEL

In a small town everyone made fun of a local misfit. They would hold out a dime and a nickel to him and ask him which he wanted. He would always choose a nickel. One day someone asked him why he always chose the nickel. The misfit replied, "If I ever took a dime, they'd quit giving me nickels."

NO

Him: There is one word that will make me the happiest man in the world. Will you marry me?

Her: No!

Him: That's the word!

NOBODY LIKES ME

"Nobody in school likes me," he complained. "The teachers don't like me, the kids don't like me, the superintendent wants to transfer me, the bus drivers hate me, the school board wants me to drop

out, and the custodians have it in for me.
I don't want to go to school."

"But you have to go to school," countered his mother. "You are healthy, you
have a lot to learn, you have something
to offer others, you are a leader. And
besides, you are 45 years old and you
are the principal."

No Bother

Nancy: Don't bother showing me to
the door.

Ned: It's no bother . . . it's a pleasure!

Not Fair

Nate: Mother, you gave brother a
bigger piece of cake than you gave me.

Mother: But, sweetheart, your brother
is a much bigger boy than you are.

Nate: Well, he always will be if this
keeps up.

Nothing to It

First preacher: I think a pastor needs
to study diligently for his Sunday morning message.

Second preacher: I disagree. Many
times I have no idea what I am going to
preach about. But I go into the pulpit
and preach, and think nothing of it.

First preacher: You are quite right in thinking nothing of it. Your deacons have told me they share your opinion.

OBJECT

He: Do you think your father would object to my marrying you?

She: I don't know. If he's anything like me, he would.

OCEAN LINERS

Q: How often do big ocean liners sink?
A: Only once.

OLD

He's so old, his first job was parking covered wagons!

• • •

Why do life insurance brokers always talk of death benefits? Growing old has its benefits. You get fewer calls from insurance salesmen.

• • •

Did you hear about the elderly couple who got married late in life? Medicare paid for the honeymoon.

• • •

You're getting on in years when you bend over to tie your laces and you look around to see if there's anything else to do while you're down there.

• • •

You know you're getting on in years if you're just as pretty as you ever were, but now it takes an hour longer.

• • •

Remember when a Saturday Night Special was a double banana split?

• • •

It takes about 20 years to get used to how old you are.

• • •

Did you hear about the young couple that swore they'd grow old together? But then something happened; he went ahead without her.

• • •

I knew I was getting old the last time I went to Las Vegas. I played a slot machine and it came up three prunes.

• • •

You know you're getting old when the happy hour is a nap.

•   •   •

You know you're getting old when you're sitting in a rocker and you can't get it started.

OLD AGE

We live in the Metal Age:
> Silver in the hair.
> Gold in the teeth.
> Lead in the pants.
> Iron in the veins.

•   •   •

The five "B's" of old age:
> Bifocals
> Bunions
> Bridges
> Bulges
> Baldness

OLD CAR

The best way to make your old car run better is to learn the price of the latest model.

OLD MAID

Old maid's laughter: He! he! he!

OLDER

As I grow older, there are three things
I have trouble remembering: faces,
names, and . . . I can't remember what
the third thing is.

ONLY GIRL

Olive: Bill told me I was the only girl
he ever loved.

Olivia: Doesn't he say it beautifully?

ON THE ROOF

A bachelor kept a cat for companion-
ship, and loved his cat more than life.
He was planning a trip to England and
entrusted the cat to his brother's care.

As soon as he arrived in England he
called his brother. "How is my cat?" he
asked. Listening intensely, he exclaimed,
"Oh my. Did you have to tell me that
way?"

"How else can I tell you your cat's
dead?" inquired the brother.

"You should have led me up to it
gradually," said the bachelor. "For
example, when I called tonight you

could have told me my cat was on the roof, but the Fire Department is getting it down. When I called tomorrow night, you could have told me they dropped him and broke his back, but a fine surgeon is doing all he can for him. Then, when I called the third night, you could have told me the surgeon did all he could but my cat passed away. That way it wouldn't have been such a shock.

"By the way," he continued, "how's Mother?"

"Mother?" came the reply. "Oh, she's up on the roof, but the Fire Department is getting her down."

OOPS

The customer wanted to buy a chicken and the butcher had only one in stock. He weighed it and said, "A beauty. That will be $1.25, lady."

"Oh, that's not quite large enough," said the customer. The butcher put the chicken back in the refrigerator, rolled it around on the ice several times, then back on the scales again.

"This one is $1.85," he said, adding his thumb for good weight.

"Oh, that's fine!" said the customer. "I'll take both of them."

OPPORTUNITY

The trouble with opportunity is that it looks bigger coming than going.

• • •

On a lonely, moonlit country road, as the car engine coughed and the car came to a halt, the following conversation took place:

"That's funny," said the young man. "I wonder what that knocking was?"

"Well, I can tell you one thing for sure," the girl answered icily. "It wasn't opportunity."

ORDERS

A salesman mentioned that he'd only gotten three orders for an entire week of work: Get out. Stay out. And don't come back.

PARADISE

Two ivory cubes with dots all over them.

PARAKEET

There's a story making the rounds that involves a carpet layer who had worked

all day installing wall-to-wall carpeting.
When he noticed a lump under the
carpet in the middle of the living room,
he felt his shirt pocket for his cigarettes—
they were gone. He was not about to
take up the carpet, so he went outside for
a two-by-four. Tampingng down the
cigarettes with it would be easy. Once
the lump was smoothed, the man
gathered up his tools and carried them to
the truck, and over his shoulder he heard
the voice of the woman to whom the
carpet belonged. "Have you seen
anything of my parakeet?" she asked
plaintively.

PARANOID

Q: How many paranoids does it take
to change a light bulb?
A: Why do you want to know?

PARAPHRASE

The teacher wrote the following
sentence on the blackboard and asked
her pupils to paraphrase it: "He was bent
on seeing her."
Little Paul turned in this paraphrase:
"The sight of her doubled him up."

PATIENCE

A customer was several months behind in paying his bill, and his last payment notice informed him that he would have to pay or the matter would be turned over to a lawyer. He responded with the following note: "Enclosed you will find a check for the entire amount. Please forgive my delay in not answering sooner. Thanks for your patience. I remain, Yours Truly . . ."

"P.S. This is the kind of letter I would write you if I had the money to pay."

PAUL REVERE

A Texan was trying to impress on a Bostonian the valor of the heroes of the Alamo. "I'll bet you never had anything so brave around Boston," said the Texan.

"Did you hear of Paul Revere?" asked the Bostonian.

"Paul Revere?" said the Texan. "Isn't he the guy who ran for help?"

PAYMENTS

Q: What goes with Early French furniture?

A: Late American payments.

PEARLS

Peter: Did you hear about the guy who brought two authentic pearl buttons from the South Sea Isle of Bali?

Pat: No, what about him?

Peter: He's the only guy in town with two pearl Bali buttons.

PEDESTRIAN

A pedestrian is what they call a father who has kids that can drive.

PERFECT AGE

My children are at the perfect age . . . too old to cry at night and too young to borrow my car.

PESSIMIST

Always borrow from a pessimist . . . he never expects it back anyhow.

PETE WILSON

Patricia: Do you know Pete Wilson?

Paul: I sure do. We slept in the same church pew for over 15 years.

PHONE NUMBER

He: If you would give me your phone number I would give you a call.

She: It's in the book.

He: Good. What is your name?

She: It's in the book, too.

PIECE OF JUNK

A collector of rare books ran into an acquaintance who had just thrown away an old Bible that had been in his family for generations. He happened to mention that Guten-something had printed it.

"Not Gutenberg?" gasped the book collector.

"Yes, that was the name."

"You idiot! You've thrown away one of the first books ever printed. A copy recently sold at auction for $400,000."

"Mine wouldn't have been worth a dime," replied the man. "Some clown by the name of Martin Luther had scribbled all over it."

PIG

Q: What do you call a pig that took an airplane ride?

A: Swine flu.

Pig Iron

Pig iron is an iron for smoothing wrinkles off pigs.

Pig Toes

In a small town the farmers of the community had gotten together to discuss some important issues. About midway through the meeting a wife of one of the farmers stood up and spoke her piece.

One old farmer, indignant, stood up and replied, "What does she know about anything. I would like to ask her if she knows how many toes a pig has?"

Quick as a flash the woman answered, "Take off your boots, man, and count them!"

Pigeon

"All right, you!" screamed the mother pigeon to her backwards squab. "Either you learn to fly today or I'll tie a rope around you and tow you."

"Oh, mother, not that!" cried her baby. "I'd rather die than be pigeon-towed."

PILOT

A little old lady called over the stewardess and told her, "Please tell the pilot not to turn on that red light. Every time he does that, it gets bumpy."

PINCH

As the crowded elevator descended, Mrs. Wilson became increasingly furious with her husband, who was delighted to be pressed against a gorgeous blonde.

As the elevator stopped at the main floor, the blonde suddenly whirled, slapped Mr. Wilson, and said, "That will teach you to pinch!"

Bewildered, Mr. Wilson was halfway to the parking lot with his wife when he choked, "I . . . I . . . didn't pinch that girl."

"Of course you didn't," said his wife, consolingly. "I did."

PLUMBER

Householder: Well, I see you brought your tools with you.

Plumber: Yeah, I'm getting more absent-minded every day.

POISON

A young mother paying a visit to a doctor friend and his wife made no attempt to restrain her five-year-old son,

who was ransacking an adjoining room.
But, finally, an extra loud chatter of
bottles prompted her to say: "I hope,
doctor, that you don't mind Peter being
in there."

"No," said the doctor calmly. "He'll be
quiet when he gets to the poisons."

POLITICIAN

The politician is my shepherd . . . I
    am in want;
He maketh me to lie down on park
    benches,
He leadeth me beside still factories;
He disturbeth my soul.
Yea, though I walk through the valley
    of the shadow of depression and
    recession,
I anticipate no recovery, for he is
    with me.
He prepareth a reduction in my salary
    in the presence of my enemies;
He anointeth my small income with
    great losses;
My expenses runneth over.
Surely unemployment and poverty
    shall follow me all the days of
    my life.
And I shall dwell in a mortgaged
    house forever.

• • •

You can always tell a good politician by the way he answers. He makes you forget the question.

● ● ●

If George Washington never told a lie, how'd he get elected?

● ● ●

Half the politicians in Washington are trying to start investigations. The other half are trying to get them stopped.

● ● ●

Politician: Well, election time will soon be here. I plan to run for office again. I guess the air will soon be full of my speeches.

Man: Yeah! . . . and vice versa!

● ● ●

The reason you will often see liberal politicians lost in deep thought is that they are so rarely in that neighborhood and usually can't find their way back home.

POPULARITY

When I asked a friend the secret of his popularity, he attributed it to one particular word. "Years ago," he said, "upon hearing a statement with which I disagreed, I used to say 'baloney,' and people avoided me like the plague. Now I substitute 'amazing' for 'baloney,' and my phone keeps ringing with invitations."

POST OFFICE

Pricilla: My brother went for a job in the post office.
Preston: What is he doing now?
Pricilla: Nothing. He got the job!

PRACTICAL PSYCHOLOGY

A mother, visiting a department store, took her son to the toy department. Spying a gigantic rocking horse, he climbed up on it and rocked back and forth for almost an hour.

"Come on, son," the mother pleaded. "I have to get home to get father's dinner."

The little lad refused to budge and all her efforts were unavailing. The department manager also tried to coax the little fellow without meeting any success. Eventually, in desperation, they called the store's psychiatrist. Gently he walked over and whispered a few words in the boy's ear and immediately the lad jumped off and ran to his mother's side.

"How did you do it?" the mother asked incredibly. "What did you say to him?"

The psychiatrist hesitated for a moment, then said, "All I said was, 'If you don't jump off that rocking horse at once, son, I'll knock the stuffing out of you!'"

PRACTICE

Daughter: Mom, may I have some money for a new dress?

Mother: Ask your father, dear. You are getting married in a month and the practice would do you good.

PREACHER

Visitor: Your preacher is sure long-winded.

Member: He may be long . . . but never winded.

PROCRASTINATION

A habit most people put off trying to correct.

PROFESSIONAL HUMORIST

One who has a good memory and hopes others haven't.

PROFIT

So this druggist is filling a prescription, hands his customer a little bottle with 12 pills in it, and says, "That'll be $4.50." Suddenly the phone rings and as the druggist turns to answer it, the customer puts 50 cents on the counter and walks out. The druggist turns back, spots the 50 cents, and yells: "Sir! Sir! That's $4.50, not 50 cents. Sir!" The guy is gone. The druggist picks up the half a buck, looks at it, shrugs, flips it into the till and mumbles: "Oh, well, 40 cents profit is better than nothing."

PSYCHIATRIST

Patty: I asked my psychiatrist, "How soon till I know I'm cured?"

Patsy: What did he say?

Patty: He said, "The day you run out of money."

• • •

Patient: Doc, I have a morbid fear of thunder.

Psychiatrist: That's silly. You shouldn't be afraid of a thing like thunder. Why don't you just think of it as a drumroll from heaven?

Patient: Will that cure me?

Psychiatrist: Well, if it doesn't, do what I did: Stuff cotton in your ears, crawl under the bed, and sing "Zippety-Doo-Dah."

• • •

Wife: My husband thinks he's a refrigerator.

Psychiatrist: I wouldn't worry as long as he is not violent.

Wife: Oh, the delusion doesn't bother me. But when he sleeps with his mouth open, the little light keeps me awake.

• • •

A psychiatrist is a person who beats a psychopath to your door.

PUMPKIN PIE

When we first married, my wife was not a very good cook. She would make new desserts and have me try them before dinner.

One day I came home and she told me she had just made a pumpkin pie. She told me to try some.

I said, "How about after dinner?"

She said, "No, I want you to try it now."

I don't want to say it was bad, but I had to drink four glassesful!

PUPS

A minister preached a very short sermon. He explained, "My dog got into my office and chewed up some of my notes."

At the close of the service a visitor asked, "If your dog ever has pups, please let my pastor have one of them."

PYRAMIDS

Teacher: Who built the pyramids?

Student: I knew, but I forgot.

Teacher: That's a shame. You're the only person alive who knows, and you had to forget.

QUICK THINKING

A Scotsman and Englishman were leaning against the counter in a store when a bandit walked in and brandished his gun.

The Scot, a quick thinker, hauled out his money and handed it to his English friend.

He said, "Here's the ten dollars you lent me."

Radical

Q: What do they call someone whose opinion differs from their own?

A: A radical.

Radio

Ralene: Were you hired by the radio station as an announcer?

Roger: N-n-no, they s-s-said I w-w-wasn't t-t-tall enough!

Rain

Mr. and Mrs. Rolls were touring Russia. Their guide's name was Rudolph, and Mr. Rolls and Rudolph argued all the time.

As the couple was leaving Moscow, the husband said, "Look, it's snowing out."

The guide disagreed, "No, sir, it's raining out."

"I still think it's snowing," said Mr. Rolls.

But his wife replied, "Rudolph the Red knows rain, dear."

Raise

Employee (shaking a little): Could I have a raise?

Manager: You can't come in here like this and ask for a raise. You've only been with the company two weeks. You have to work yourself up first.

Employee: But I did...look...I'm trembling all over!

• • •

Employee: I have been here 11 years doing three men's work for one man's pay. Now I want a raise.

Boss: Well, I can't give you a raise, but if you'll tell me who the other two men are, I'll fire them.

Raising Hogs

Letter sent to the Secretary of Agriculture
Dear Mr. Secretary:

My friend Bordereaux received a $1,000 check from the government for not raising hogs, and so I am going into the not-raising-hogs business.

What I want to know is, what is the best kind of land not to raise hogs on, and what is the best kind of hog not to raise? I would prefer not to raise razorbacks, but if this is not the best kind not to raise, I will just as gladly not raise durocs or Poland Chinas.

The hardest part of this business is going to be keeping an individual record on each of the hogs I do not raise.

My friend Bordereaux has been raising hogs for more than 20 years and the most he ever made was $400 in 1918, until this year when he received $1,000 for not raising hogs. Now, if I get $1,000 for not raising 50 hogs, I will get $2,000 for not raising 100 hogs, and so on.

I plan to start off on a small scale, holding myself down to not raising 4,000 hogs for which I will, of course, receive $80,000.

Now, these hogs I will not raise will not eat 100,000 bushels of corn. I understand that you pay farmers for not raising corn. Will you pay me for not raising 100,000 bushels of corn, which I will not feed to the hogs which I am not raising?

I want to get started as soon as possible, as this looks like a good time of year for not raising hogs.

Yours very truly,
Octover Brussard

RAW OYSTERS

Customer: I'll have some raw oysters, not too large nor too small, not too salty nor too fat. They must be cold, and I want them quickly!

Waiter: Yes, sir! With or without pearls?

REAL SMART

"Your methods of farming are out-of-date," said an agricultural student to an old farmer. "I'd be surprised if you got eight pounds of oranges off that tree."

"So would I," said the old farmer. "That's a pear tree."

REFUSE

"If you refuse to marry me I will die," said the young romantic. And, sure enough, 50 years later he died.

REPAIRS

The owner of the electronics store was showing the new salesman around. "We buy these VCRs for $30 and sell them for $29.95."

"Twenty-Nine Ninety-Five!" exclaimed the new man. "How do you make any money?"

"That comes when we repair them."

RESTITUTION

A home for chronically exhausted people.

RICH

Ronald: Could you tell me how you became such a rich man?

Rick: Turn out the lights and I will tell you the story.

Ronald: You need not tell the story. I think I already know.

RINGING IN THE EARS

A man sought medical aid because he had popped eyes and a ringing in the ears. A doctor looked him over and suggested removal of his tonsils. The operation resulted in no improvement, however, so the patient consulted another doctor who suggested removal of his teeth. The teeth were extracted, but still the man's eyes popped and the ringing in his ears continued.

A third doctor told him bluntly, "You've got six months to live." In that event, the doomed man decided he'd treat himself right while he could. He bought a flashy car, a chauffeur, had the best tailor in town make him 30 suits, and decided even his shirts would be made-to-order.

"Okay," said the shirtmaker, "let's get your measurement. Hmm, 34 sleeve, 16 collar."

"Fifteen," the man said.

"Sixteen collar," the shirtmaker repeated, measuring again. "If you wear a shirt too tight, your eyes will pop and you will hear a ringing in your ears."

ROBBERY

Q: What kind of robbery may not be dangerous?

A: A safe robbery.

ROOSTER

Q: What is the difference between a rooster, Uncle Sam, and an old maid?

A: The rooster says, "Cock-a-doodle-doo"; Uncle Sam says, "Yankee-doodle-doo"; and an old maid says, "Any dude'll do."

RUSSIA

In Russia, there's a shortage of everything but shortages.

SALARY

Sam: Did you know that some of the presidents gave their salaries back to the government?

Steve: That idea really caught on. Now they have us all doing it.

• • •

Note inside of pay envelope:
EMPLOYEES SHOULD NOT DISCUSS THEIR
SALARIES WITH OTHERS.

The employee replied, "Don't worry!
I'm as ashamed of it as you are."

SALE

Business was pretty bad at Swade's
Bargain Emporium. Then, to compound
his troubles, Sal's on his right decided
to run a big going-out-of-business sale
and hung up a sign reading, THE GREAT-
EST GOING-OUT OF-BUSINESS SALE EVER.
YOU COULDN'T GET BIGGER BARGAINS
IF WE WERE REALLY GOING OUT OF
BUSINESS.

Then Scott's, on Sal's left, decided to
run a sale and hung up a sign reading,
FIRE SALE. YOU COULDN'T GET BETTER
BUYS EVEN IF THERE WAS A REAL FIRE.

Swade joined the fun. He hung up a
sign directly between the others reading,
ENTRANCE TO SALE.

SANTA CLAUS

Santa Claus is a person who does not
come through the chimney. He comes
through a large hole in your pocketbook.

SAVINGS AND LOAN

Did you hear about the couple that had only two children? The first is the president of a savings and loan, and the other one is in jail too.

SCHIZOPHRENIC

A patient went to his doctor and said, "I'm feeling very schizophrenic today."

The doctor said, "That makes four of us."

SCRAMBLED

A psychiatrist was trying to comfort a new patient who was terribly upset. "You see, doc," the patient explained, "My problem is that I like shoes much better than I like boots."

"Why, that's no problem," answered the doctor. "Most people like shoes better than boots."

The patient was elated, "That's neat, doc. How do you like them, fried or scrambled?"

SEAFOOD DIET

My husband is on a seafood diet. Every time he sees food, he eats.

SEASICK

Steward: Shall I send you some dinner, sir?

Seasick man: No, just throw it overboard and save me the trouble.

SECRET

Young man: May I ask you the secret of your success?

Executive: There is no easy secret. You just jump at your opportunity.

Young man: But how can I tell when my opportunity comes?

Executive: You can't, you have to keep on jumping.

SENSIBLE

Boy: You look like a sensible girl. Let's get married.

Girl: Nothing doing. I'm just as sensible as I look.

SERMON

First Member: I thought the sermon was divine. It reminded me of the peace of God. It passed all understanding.

Second Member: It reminded me of the mercies of God. I thought it would endure forever.

• • •

Student: Does a good beginning and a good ending make a good sermon?

Professor: If they're close enough together.

SEVEN AGES

The seven ages of a woman are baby, child, girl, young woman, young woman, young woman, and poised social leader.

SHAMPOO

"What happened to the other barber that used to be here?"

"Well, he is now in a home for the insane. His business was slow, and one day he asked a customer if he wanted a shampoo. The customer said, 'No.' I guess that was the last straw. He took a razor and slashed the customer's throat. By the way, how about a shampoo today?"

"Sure, go ahead," said the customer.

SHOCK TREATMENT

The latest thing in shock treatment is a psychiatrist who sends his bills in advance.

SHOOT

Robber: I'm going to shoot you.
Man: Why?
Robber: I shoot anyone who looks like me.
Man: Do I look like you?
Robber: Yes.
Man: Then shoot.

SHRINK

If you wonder why a psychiatrist is called a "shrink," check your bank account after a month.

• • •

You can go to a shrink slightly cracked, and before you get done, you're broke.

• • •

A patient lies down on the couch, and the shrink says, "Okay, tell me what you dreamed last night."
"I didn't dream."
"How can I help you if you don't do your homework?"

SIAMESE TWINS

Sean: I just had a date with some Siamese twins.

Shane: Did you have a good time?
Sean: Yes and no.

SICK

Steven: Mrs. Stalls, may I look at
your rug?

Mrs. Stalls: Why, of course, Steven.
Come in.

Steven: I don't understand . . . it
doesn't make me sick.

SIDE ACHE

After hearing the story about how
God took the rib out of Adam's side, a
little boy who had been running and had
a side ache said to his mother, "I think
I'm going to have a wife."

SIGHTS

Sara: And what brings you to town?

Sally: I just came to see the sights, and
I thought I'd call on you first.

SIGN

Boy: You look prettier every minute.
Do you know what that is a sign of?

Girl: Yes, you are about to run out
of gas.

SINGER

Hostess: That singer has a terrible voice. Do you know who she is?

Man: Yes, she is my wife.

SINGING

Wife: Why do you go on the balcony when I sing? Don't you like to hear me?

Husband: I want the neighbors to see I'm not beating my wife.

• • •

A song leader had a very rough time when he was leading and didn't notice the words of the song. He said, "I want the women to sing the verse, 'I will go home today,' and the men to come in on the chorus with 'Glad day, Glad day.'" The people were laughing too much to sing the song.

SKI PANTS

Those stretch ski pants come in three sizes: small, medium, and don't bend over.

SMALL

Son: I'm supposed to tell you that there will be a small Parent-Teachers meeting tomorrow night.

Father: Well, if it's going to be small, do I have to go?

Son: Oh, yes! It's just you, me, the teacher, and the principal.

SMALL TOWN

If nobody knows the trouble you've seen, then you don't live in a small town.

SMART MAN

At a reception in Washington, a young man was asked by a widow to guess her age. "You must have some idea," she said, as he hesitated.

"I have several ideas," he admitted, with a smile. "The trouble is that I hesitate whether to make it ten years younger on account of your looks or ten years older on account of your intelligence."

SMILES

Stan: Did you see that young lady smile at me?

Stew: That's nothing. The first time I saw you, I laughed right out loud.

SMOKING

Stacey: Did you hear about the man who read that smoking was bad for your health?

Stanley: No. What about him?

Stacey: He immediately gave up reading.

SNORING

Why is it that the loudest snorer is always the first one to go to sleep?

SNOW WHITE

Q: What did Snow White say when her pictures did not arrive back from the photo service?

A: Someday my prints will come.

SOFTWARE

Q: How many software programmers does it take to screw in a light bulb?

A: None. It's a hardware problem.

SOUND THINKER

A sound thinker is someone whose opinions coincide with your own.

SPEAKER

Recently, our speaker had to discontinue several of his long talks on account of his throat. Several people threatened to cut it.

SPECIAL REDUCING DIET

Monday
Breakfast–Weak tea
Lunch–1 bouillon cube in 1/2 cup diluted water
Dinner–1 pigeon thigh, 72 oz. prune juice (gargle only)

Tuesday
Breakfast–Scraped crumbs from burned toast
Lunch–1 doughnut hole (without sugar)
Dinner–2 jellyfish skins and 1 glass dehydrated water

Wednesday
Breakfast–Boiled out stains from table cover
Lunch–1/2 dozen poppy seeds
Dinner–Bee knees and mosquito knuckles sauteed with vinegar

Thursday
Breakfast–Shredded eggshell skins

Lunch—Bellybutton from a naval orange

Dinner—3 eyes from Irish potatoes (diced)

Friday

Breakfast—2 lobster antennae and 1 guppy fin

Lunch—1 guppy fin

Dinner—Jellyfish vertebrae a la book binders

Saturday

Breakfast—4 chopped banana seeds

Lunch—Broiled butterfly liver

Dinner—Fillet of soft shell crab slaw

Sunday

Breakfast—Pickled hummingbird tongue

Lunch—Prime ribs of tadpole and aroma of empty custard pie plate

Dinner Tossed paprika and clover leaf (1) salad

SPEECH

Chauncey Depew once played a trick on Mark Twain on an occasion when they were both to speak at a banquet. Twain spoke first for some 20 minutes and was received with great enthusiasm. When Depew's turn came immediately afterward, he said, "Mr. Toastmaster,

Ladies and Gentlemen, before this
dinner, Mark Twain and I made an
agreement to trade speeches. He has just
delivered mine and I'm grateful for the
reception you have accorded it. I regret
that I have lost his speech and cannot
remember a thing he had to say."

He sat down with much applause.

SPEED LIMIT

Nothing is more exasperating than
getting behind a guy in the lane who is
observing the speed limit.

SPINACH

Mother: Eat your spinach. Think of
the thousands of starving children who
would love some spinach like this.

Son: Name two.

SPLIT SECOND

Q: What do they call the interval from
the time the traffic light turns green until
the guy behind you honks his horn?

A: A split second.

SQUAWS

There were three Indian squaws, one
sitting on an elk hide, one on a deer

hide, and one on a hippopotamus hide. The two squaws on the elk and deer hides had one papoose each, while the squaw on the hippopotamus hide had two papooses.

Moral: The squaw on the hippopotamus equals the sum of the squaws on the other two hides.

STAR SPANGLED BANNER

Immigration men are clever guys. This one fellow in particular has a little trick. He asks, "What's your nationality?"

"American."

"American, huh? Do you know the words of 'The Star Spangled Banner'?"

"No, I don't."

"You're an American: go in."

STATIONERY STORE

A store that stays pretty much at the same location.

STEALING

Did you hear about the man who was brought in for stealing a pair of shoes? The judge said, "Weren't you here last year for the same charge?"

The man replied, "Your Honor, how long can a pair of shoes last?"

• • •

The manager of a supermarket accidentally overheard a man bragging about how much he'd been stealing from the store. When the man came in the next day, the manager followed him around. The man loaded his cart, paid for every item, and put the groceries in his car.

In the weeks that followed, the man kept returning to shop. A dozen times he loaded his cart with groceries, and a dozen times he paid for every single item.

Finally, the manager walked over to him and said, "Mister, I've been watching you like a hawk. I've never seen you pocket one thing. You've never hidden anything under your coat. And you've paid for every item you've bought. Look, I won't prosecute or say a word. In fact, I'll give you a hundred dollars if you tell me what you're stealing."

The man said, "Shopping carts."

STEAMROLLER

Did you hear about the man who was run over by a steamroller? His doctor told him to stay flat on his back.

ST. GEORGE

A tramp knocked on the door of the inn known as St. George and the Dragon. The landlady opened the door, and the tramp asked, "Could you give a poor man something to eat?"

"No!" replied the woman, slamming the door in his face.

A few minutes later the tramp knocked again. The landlady came to the door again. This time the tramp asked, "Could I have a few words with George?"

STOCK MARKET

Sally: Did you hear Steve made a killing in the stock market?
Sara: No, really?
Sally: Yeah, he shot his broker!

STRANGE AND WONDERFUL

We have a strange and wonderful relationship. He's strange and I'm wonderful.

STRIKING SERMON

A striking sermon is one that hits the man who is not there.

STUCCO

Stucco is what you get when you sit on gummo.

SUCCESS

Young doctor: What is the secret of your success?

Old doctor: Always write your prescriptions illegibly and your bills very plainly.

• • •

Rookie: How did you become such a successful door-to-door salesman?

Salesman: It's all because of the first five words I utter when a woman opens the door. 'Miss, is your mother in?'"

SUNBURN

Q: What do you call a sunburn on your stomach?

A: A pot roast.

SUNDAY SCHOOL

Overheard after Sunday school:

"Is it true that shepherds have dirty socks?"

"What do you mean?"

"I heard that the shepherds washed their socks by night."

● ● ●

Teacher: What parable in the Bible do you like best?

Student: The one about the fellow that loafs and fishes.

SYNONYM

Teacher: Scotty, what is a synonym?

Scotty: A synonym is a word you use when you can't spell the other one.

TAKE OVER

Husband: I know you are having a lot of trouble with the baby, dear, but keep in mind, "the hand that rocks the cradle is the hand that rules the world."

Wife: How about taking over the world for a few hours while I go shopping.

TALKING

Mother: Tina, I have told you before not to speak when older people are talking. Wait until they stop.

Tina: I tried, but they never stop.

TAXES

It's becoming more and more difficult to support the government in the style to which it has become accustomed.

• • •

A man walked into the tax collector's office and sat down and smiled at everyone.

"May I help you?" said the clerk in charge.

"No," said the man. "I just wanted to meet the people I have been working for all these years."

• • •

I'm a little worried about this year's income tax. I think I made it out wrong. I've got 42 cents left.

• • •

Don't be surprised if your next income tax form is simplified to contain only four lines:

1. What was your income last year?
2. What were your expenses?
3. How much do you have left?
4. Send it in.

TAXI

Q: What do they call cabs lined up at the Dallas airport?

A: The yellow rows of taxis.

TAXPAYERS

People who don't have to take a civil service test to work for the government.

TEAMWORK

Panting and perspiring, two men on a tandem bicycle at last get to the top of a steep hill.

"That was a stiff climb," said the first man.

"It certainly was," replied the second man. "And if I hadn't kept the brake on, we would have slid down backwards."

TEE-BAGS

"We're going to serve as caddies-for-a-day at the country club, but don't know what to call ourselves. We've thought of Caddie-etts, and Link Lassies, but we need something more original."

"I have it," offered her husband. "How about Tee-Bags?"

TEENAGER

Father to teenage son: Do you mind if I use the car tonight?

Teenage son: Ah, Dad, tonight?

Father: Well, I'm taking your mother out, and I would like to impress her.

• • •

My son's room is so dirty, he just got an EPA grant to clean it up.

TELEVISION

Television must be bad. I came home the other night, and my kid was doing homework.

TEMPERAMENTAL

Ninety percent temper; ten percent mental.

TENNIS

Discussing his tennis technique, a stout, bald man panted: "My brain immediately barks out a command to my body. 'Run forward, but fast,' it says. 'Start right now. Drop the ball gracefully over the net and then walk back slowly.'"

"And then what happens?" asked a friend.

"And then my body asks, 'Who, me?'"

TENNIS BALLS

Sign in sporting goods store:
SALE ON TENNIS BALLS. FIRST COME, FIRST SERVE.

TERMITE

Scientists have just crossed a termite with a praying mantis. Now they have a termite that says grace before it eats your house.

TERROR

Mother: Every time you're naughty I get another gray hair.

Son: Gee, Mom, you must have been a terror when you were young . . . just look at Grandma.

TEXAN

A Texas rancher was visiting an Iowa farm. The Iowa farmer was justly proud of his 200 acres of rich, productive land.

"Is this your whole farm?" the Texan asked. "Why back in Texas I get in my truck at 5:00 in the morning, and I drive and drive all day. At dusk I just reach the other end of my ranch."

The Iowa farmer thought a while and replied, "I used to have a truck like that too."

THE ISMS

Communism: If you have two cows, you give both cows to the government, and then the government sells you some of the milk.

Socialism: If you have two cows, you give both cows to the government, and then the government gives you some of the milk.

Naziism: If you have two cows, the government shoots you and takes both cows.

Facism: If you have two cows, you milk both of them and give the government half of the milk.

New Dealism: If you have two cows, you kill one, milk the other, and pour the milk down the drain.

Capitalism: If you have two cows, you sell one cow and buy a bull.

THIEF

A person who is in the habit of finding things before the owner loses them.

THREE CAMELS

Noah was standing at the gangplank checking off the pairs of animals when he saw three camels trying to get on board. "Wait a minute!" said Noah. "Two each is the limit. One of you will have to stay behind."

"It won't be me," said the first camel. "I'm the camel whose back is broken by the last straw."

"I'm the one people swallow while straining at a gnat," said the second.

"I," said the third, "am the one that shall pass through the eye of a needle sooner than a rich man shall enter heaven."

"Come on in," said Noah, "the world is going to need all of you."

THREE ENVELOPES

The head of sales was leaving and being replaced by Gilbert, a younger manager. As the retiring executive met Gilbert for the last time, he handed him three sealed envelopes.

"I'm going to do for you what my predecessor did for me, Gilbert. Here are three numbered envelopes. When you run into your first crisis, open the first envelope. When you hit the second major problem, open the next. Save the last envelope for the third crisis. And good luck."

Then he left.

When the first half-year dividend was declared, it was just a fraction of the previous year's earnings. The CEO was furious and demanded an immediate report from every department head. Gilbert realized it was time for action. He opened his desk drawer and ripped open the first envelope.

BLAME YOUR PREDECESSOR

When he met with the CEO the next day, he followed the letter's advice and tore into the man he had replaced. The CEO was satisfied.

Six months later, the year-end sales figures were posted. The numbers were just half the previous year's. Again, the CEO was furious and demanded an explanation. Gilbert hurried back to his office and, with trembling hands, opened envelope number two.

REORGANIZE

Following the advice, he presented a new departmental structure and organizational chart to the CEO. New people were to be hired and a dozen were to be replaced. The CEO was happy.

Another six months went by and the new people were producing even less than the old employees. Sales were still down and morale was terrible. The CEO called and in a gruff voice barked, "Get yourself down here, Gilbert." It was time for the last envelope, which he hurriedly opened and read.

PREPARE THREE ENVELOPES . . .

TIGER

Q: What is the difference between a tiger and a comma?

A: The tiger has claws at the end of his paws, and the comma is a pause at the end of a clause.

TIP

Customer: I am sorry, waiter, but I only have enough money for the bill. I have nothing left for a tip.

Waiter: Let me add up that bill again, sir.

TIRED

I just found out why I feel tired all the time. We did a survey and found I was doing more than my share of the world's work.

The population of the country is 160 million, but there are 62 million over 60 years of age. That leaves 98 million to do the work. People under 21 years of age total 54 million, which leaves 44 million to do the work.

Then there are 21 million who are employed by the government and that leaves 23 million to do the work. Ten million are in the armed forces. That leaves 13 million to do the work. Now deduct 12,800,000—the number in state and city offices—and that leaves 200,000 to do the work. There are 126,000 in hospitals, insane asylums, and so forth, and that leaves 74,000 people to do the work.

But 62,000 of these refuse to work, so that leaves 12,000 to do the work. Now it may interest you to know that there are 11,988 people in jail, so that leaves just two people to do all the work and that's YOU and ME and I'm getting tired doing everything myself.

TOMORROW

Ken: There's nothing like getting up at five in the morning and taking an ice-cold shower and a five-mile jog before breakfast.

Bob: How long have you been doing this?

Ken: I start tomorrow.

TOOTH FAIRY

We were so poor, the tooth fairy used to leave us IOUs!

TOOTHPASTE

Terry: Did you hear about the new toothpaste that has shoe polish in it?

Toby: No I haven't, tell me about it.

Terry: It is for people who put their foot in their mouth.

TRACKER

A man walking along the road saw a tracker lying with his ear to the ground. He went over and listened. The tracker said, "Large wheels, Ford pickup truck, green color, man driving with large police dog next to him, Colorado license plate, and traveling about 75 miles per hour."

The man was astounded. "You mean you can tell all that just by listening with your ear to the ground?" he asked.

"Ear to the ground, nothing," said the tracker. "That truck just ran over me."

TRANQUILIZERS

Malpractice insurance is what allows people to be ill at ease.

TRIPLETS

Doctor: Did you tell Mr. Teeves that he is the father of triplets?

Nurse: No, he is still shaving.

TROUBLES

Remember this before you burden other people with your troubles. Half of them aren't the least bit interested, and the rest are delighted that you're getting what they think is coming to you.

• • •

So you think you have troubles! When I got to the building, I found that the hurricane had knocked some bricks off the top. So I rigged up a beam with a pulley at the top of the building and hoisted up a couple of barrels full of bricks. When I had fixed the building, there were a lot of bricks left over. Then I went to the bottom of the building and cast off the line. Unfortunately, the barrel of bricks was heavier than I was, and before I knew what was happening, the barrel started down, jerking me off the ground. I decided to hang on and halfway up I met the barrel coming down and received a hard blow on the shoulder.

I then continued to the top, banging my head against the beam and getting my fingers jammed in the pulley. When the barrel hit the ground it burst its bottom, allowing all the bricks to spill out. I was now heavier than the barrel and so started down again at high speed.

Halfway down I met the barrel coming up and received more injuries to my shins. When I hit the ground, I landed on the bricks, getting several painful cuts.

At this point I must have lost my presence of mind because I let go of the line. The barrel came down, giving me another heavy blow on the head and putting me in the hospital.

I respectfully request sick leave.

TRY AGAIN

Off the coast of Oregon, a ship collided with a fishing boat in heavy fog. No real damage was done, but as the offending ship tried to back off, it banged into the boat again. The captain was afraid he might have done some damage with the second blow. "Can you stay afloat?" he shouted through a megaphone to the floundering victim.

"I guess so," called back the skipper of the boat. "Do you want to try again?"

TULIPS

Tulips are the standard number of lips assigned to each person.

TV

Husband: Why do you weep and snuffle over a TV program and the imaginary woes of people you have never met?

Wife: For the same reason you scream and yell when a man you don't know makes a touchdown.

VACATION

A traveling salesman was held up in the West by a storm and flood. He wired his office in New York: DELAYED BY STORM. SEND INSTRUCTIONS.

His boss wired back: COMMENCE VACATION IMMEDIATELY.

VISIT

A minister habitually told his congregation that if they needed a pastoral visit they should drop a note in the offering plate. One evening after services he discovered a note that said: "I am one of your loneliest members and heaviest contributors. May I have a visit tomorrow evening?" It was signed by his wife.

VISITING

I enjoy visiting my friends so I can look at my library and all my garden tools.

WAITING

Every chair in the doctor's waiting room was filled and some patients were standing. At one point the conversation died down and there was silence. During the silence an old man stood up wearily and remarked, "Well, I guess I'll go home and die a natural death."

WARM

The people in Los Angeles aren't very warm. If it weren't for the muggings, there'd be no personal contact at all.

WASTE DUMP

Q: How many people does it take to clean up a waste dump?

A: Exactly 100. One tractor driver to handle the hazardous waste and 99 environmental lawyers to handle the toxic lawsuits.

Water on the Knee

Did you hear about the woman who had water on the knee? She got rid of it by wearing pumps.

Weather

Don't knock the weather. Nine-tenths of the people couldn't start a conversation if it didn't change once in a while.

Well-Informed

You can always tell when a man's well-informed. His views are pretty much like your own.

Where Is He Going?

The average man's life consists of 20 years of having his mother ask him where he is going; 40 years of having his wife ask the same question; and at the end, the mourners wonder too.

Who Is It?

Once upon a time there was a parrot who could say only three little words: "Who is it?" One day when the parrot was alone in the house, there was a loud knock on the door. "Who is it?" screeched the parrot.

"It's the plumber," the visitor responded.

"Who is it?" repeated the parrot.

"It's the plumber, I tell you," was the reply. "You called me to tell me your cellar was flooded."

Again the parrot called, "Who is it?"

By this time, the plumber became so angry that he fainted. A neighbor rushed over to see the cause of the commotion and found the visitor had died because of a heart attack. He looked at the man and said, "Who is it?" The parrot answered, "It's the plumber!"

WHO PAYS THE BILL?

In reply to your request to send a check, I wish to inform you that the present condition of my bank account makes it almost impossible.

My shattered financial condition is due to federal laws, corporation laws, mothers-in-law, brothers-in-law, sisters-in-law, and outlaws.

Through these taxes I am compelled to pay a business tax, assessment tax, head tax, school tax, income tax, casket tax, food tax, furniture tax, sales tax, and excise tax. Even my brain is taxed.

I am required to get a business license, car license, hunting license, fishing license, truck and auto license, not to mention marriage and dog license. I am also required to contribute to every society and organization which the genius of man is capable of bringing into life; to women's relief, unemployed relief, and gold digger's relief—also to every hospital and charitable institution in the city, including the Red Cross, the Black Cross, the Purple Cross, and the Double Cross.

For my own safety, I am compelled to carry life insurance, liability insurance, burglary insurance, accident insurance, property insurance, business insurance, earthquake insurance, tornado insurance, unemployment insurance, old age insurance, and fire insurance.

My own business is so governed that it is no easy matter for me to find out who owns it. I am inspected, suspected, disrespected, rejected, dejected, and compelled until I prove an inexhaustible supply of money for every known need of the human race.

Simply because I refuse to donate something or other I am boycotted, talked about, lied about, held up, held down, and robbed until I am almost ruined. I can tell you honestly that except for a miracle that happened I could not enclose this check. The wolf that comes to my door nowadays just had pups in my kitchen. I sold them, and here's the money.

Would like more business to pay more taxes.

Sincerely yours,

WIFE

Employee: Sir, my wife . . . er . . . told me I must ask for an increase.

Employer: Well, I'll ask my wife if I can give you one.

WILL

The town's richest man was being interviewed by a reporter for the local paper. "I owe all my success to a strong will," said the rich man.

"Your strong will?" asked the reporter.

"Not mine, my father's. He died and left me everything in his will."

WINDMILL

A tourist saw his first country windmill and asked the farmer what it was. The farmer said, "It's an electric fan for blowing the flies off my cows."

WINNER

Customer: One of the claws on the lobster is missing.

Waiter: Well, they fight in the kitchen and sometimes bite each other's claws off.

Customer: Then take this one back and bring me a winner.

WITS

Wane: I have had to make a living by my wits.

Will: Well, half a living is better than none.

WORK

The computer salesman was showing the businessman a new machine. "With the executive software program loaded into this computer, it will cut your secretary's workload in half."

"Good. I'll take two."

• • •

Boss: Waters, how long have you been working here?

Waters: Ever since I heard you coming down the hall.

• • •

Q: What is it that has never killed anybody, but seems to scare some people half to death?

A: Work.

WORLD'S BEST AFTER-DINNER SPEECH

Waiter, give me both checks.

WORRY

Walter: I'd give a thousand dollars to anyone who would do my worrying for me.

Wade: You're on. Where's the thousand?

Walter: That's your first worry.

WRECK

Two truck drivers applied for a job. One said, "I'm Pete, and this is my partner Mike; when I drive at night, he sleeps."

The foreman said, "All right, I'll give you an oral test. It's three o'clock in the morning. You're on a little bridge and your truck is loaded with nitroglycerin. All of a sudden a truck comes toward you at about 80 miles per hour. What's the first thing you do?"

"I wake up my partner Mike . . . He never saw a wreck like this before."

WRITER

A young writer sent a manuscript to a famous author along with a note saying, "Please read this manuscript and advise. Please answer as quickly as possible because I have other irons in the fire."

The noted writer sent back a brief note that said, "Remove irons. Insert manuscript."

YELLOW

A young man wrote a note to his girl-friend that said, "If you love me, wear a red rose in your corsage tonight at the play. If my devotion to you is hopeless, wear a white rose." She wore a yellow rose.

Index

Bore

Boring

Boss

Bowler

Brat

Breath

Bright Idea

Bubble Gum

Bucket Seats

Buffalo

Business

Calf

Cancer

Candles

Capital Punishment

Car

Car Sickness

Carburetor

Cards

Career

Carp

Cash

Cavity

Cement

Chaos

Cheapskate

Chicken

Childish Games

Chimney Sweep

Chronic Fatigue

Cigar

Cigarette

Clergyman

Clever

Cobweb

Coincidence

Cold Cuts

Collection

Collector

College-Bred

Complaining

Conceited

Conclusion

Confidence

Congress

Conscience

Consultation

Counterfeit

Courage

Crazy

Credit

Creditors

Crime

Criminal Lawyer

Critic

Crook

Cruise

Cupid

Curiosity

Day Off

Deacon

Debts

Decisions

Democrats

Dentist

Depression

Dermatologist

Detour

Diamond Jubilee

Diet

Dieter's Psalm

Dinner

Dishes

Dizzy

Doctor

Dollar

Dopey Blonde

Draftsman

Drums

Dull

Duties

Effective

Egotist

Elephants

Embarrass

Embarrassing

Enemy

Engagement

Engagement Ring

Eureka

Excuse Me

Executive

Exercise

Faint

False Teeth

Famous Last Words

Fancy

Farmer

Fast

Fast-Food

Fast Learner

Father's Day

Fern

Filing Cabinet

Flabbergasted

Flatterer

Flat Tire

Flooded

Fodder
Football
Forgery
Fortune
Fortuneteller
Freedom
Freeway
Gambling
Gangster
Garage Sale
Geronimo
Get-Up-and-Go
Girdle Manufacturer
Giving
Glaciers
Going Out of Business
Golf
Good Catch
Good for Society
Gossip
Gotcha
Government
Grandparent
Grass House
Grave
Grouch
Growing Old

Growing Up
Guests
Half-Wit
Hammer from Sears
Happiness
Happy
Hari-Kari
Health
Help Yourself
High Society
Hiss
Hobbies
Hold It
Hollywood
Honest
Honesty
Horse Doctor
Horse Sense
Hours
Housewarming
Housewife
Howling Success
Huck & Finn
Hungry
Hunter
Hunting
Ideas

Idiot

Imagination

I'm Fine

Improvement

Insane

Insane Asylum

Insanity

International Conscience

Introduction

IRS

Jealousy

Jogging

Joint Checking Account

Joke

Joneses

Judge

Junk

Jury Duty

Kamikaze

Kingdom

King Midas

Kiss

Kissing

Kite

Knock, Knock

Laplander

Late

Latin

Laugh

Laughter

Lawyer

Lending

Liberal

Librarian

Life Insurance

Living Room

Locomotive

Lord's Prayer

Louder

Love

Lunatics

Map

Marbles

Margie

Mark

Marriage

Marry

Matrimony

Medicare

Megavitamins

Melody in F

Memory

Merits

Middle-Aged

Mind	Not Fair
Minister	Nothing To It
Miserable	Object
Monkey	Ocean Liners
Monologue	Old
Moon	Old Age
Mountain Climbing	Old Car
Mousetrap	Old Maid
Movers and Shakers	Older
Movie Theater	Only Girl
Muggers	On the Roof
Mugwump	Oops
Music	Opportunity
My Wife	Orders
Napoleon	Paradise
Narrow Escape	Parakeet
Natural	Paranoid
Nature	Paraphrase
Neatness	Patience
Nerve	Paul Revere
Nervous	Payments
Nervous Breakdown	Pearls
Newlyweds	Pedestrian
Nickel	Perfect Age
No	Pessimist
Nobody Likes Me	Pete Wilson
No Bother	Phone Number

Piece of Junk

Pig

Pig Iron

Pig Toes

Pigcon

Pilot

Pinch

Plumber

Poison

Politician

Popularity

Post Office

Practical Psychology

Practice

Preacher

Procrastination

Professional Humorist

Profit

Psychiatrist

Pumpkin Pie

Pups

Pyramids

Quick Thinking

Radical

Radio

Rain

Raise

Raising Hogs

Raw Oysters

Real Smart

Refuse

Repairs

Restitution

Rich

Ringing in the Ears

Robbery

Rooster

Russia

Salary

Sale

Santa Claus

Savings and Loan

Schizophrenic

Scrambled

Seafood Diet

Seasick

Secret

Sensible

Sermon

Seven Ages

Shampoo

Shock Treatment

Shoot

Shrink

Siamese Twins

Sick

Side Ache

Sights

Sign

Singer

Singing

Ski Pants

Small

Small Town

Smart Man

Smiles

Smoking

Snoring

Snow White

Software

Sound Thinker

Speaker

Special Reducing Diet

Speech

Speed Limit

Spinach

Split Second

Squaws

Star Spangled Banner

Stationery Store

Stealing

Steamroller

St. George

Stock Market

Strange and Wonderful

Striking Sermon

Stucco

Success

Sunburn

Sunday School

Synonym

Take Over

Talking

Taxes

Taxi

Taxpayers

Teamwork

Tee-Bags

Teenager

Television

Temperamental

Tennis

Tennis Balls

Termite

Terror

Texan

The Isms

Thief

Three Camels
Three Envelopes
Tiger
Tip
Tired
Tongue Sandwich
Tooth Fairy
Toothpaste
Tracker
Tranquilizers
Triplets
Troubles
Try Again
Tulips
TV
Vacation
Visit
Visiting
Waiting
Warm
Waste Dump
Water on the Knee
Weather
Well-Informed
Where Is He Going?
Who Is It?
Who Pays the Bill?

Wife
Will
Windmill
Winner
Wits
Work
World's Best After-
    Dinner Speech
Worry
Wreck
Writer
Yellow